THE GREAT OCEAN ROAD

GREAT OCEAN PUBLICATIONS

PHOTOGRAPHED AND WRITTEN BY RODNEY HYETT

QUEENSCLIFF

A popular seaside resort during the late nineteenth century, Queenscliff has been restored to its former glory by way of the sumptuous restoration of its older hotels. Situated on a narrow headland within Port Phillip Bay, the township is surrounded by calm waters and it is therefore surprising that it should have a lighthouse at all, let alone two magnificent specimens. In fact, they are necessary indicators for a ship's safe passage through Port Phillip Heads, assisted by pilot boats based at Queenscliff. Historically this area was of strategic importance for naval defence, dating back to 1860 when three 68 pounder cannons were placed on the cliff top in response to fears of a Russian invasion. The Black Lighthouse was constructed from bluestone in 1863 and the fort that encloses it was completed in 1884. It is a little known fact that the first artillery shot fired by the British Empire in World War One was on order from Fort Queenscliff. From across the bay, at Point Nepean, the shot was aimed over the stern of a German freighter escaping the bay. A military museum is now located within the fort. Swan Bay, on the northern side of Queenscliff, is a Marine National Park and home to the new Marine Discovery Centre. Close to the shoreline, it is an architectural masterpiece of understatement, yet at the same time, resounding in its ecologically sensitive design and construction. It serves the dual purpose of state government marine research facility and educational display open to the public. Another informative tourist attraction is the Maritime Museum located close to the wharf. Apart from the pilot boats, the wharf (currently undergoing extensive redevelopment) is home to a substantial fishing fleet and ferry service to Sorrento, all in all creating a focus of activity for the township and its stream of sea-borne visitors.

TOP: Gracious buildings of the late nineteenth century. BOTTOM: The Black Lighthouse located within Fort Queenscliff. OPPOSITE: Shortland's Bluff and the Black Lighthouse.

Nestled behind sand dunes and amongst thick tea tree, Point Lonsdale is positioned on Port Phillip Heads overlooking the notorious Rip, through which all Melbourne and Geelong shipping must pass. The most conspicuous landmark is the lighthouse which is manned 24 hours a day and controls all traffic through the heads, which is about 20 commercial ships daily. Just below the lighthouse is Buckley's Cave which was supposedly the home of William Buckley in the early 1800s. He escaped from a convict settlement at Sorrento in 1803, aged 23, and spent 32 years dwelling with the local aborigines in the region. (An account of his ordeal begins on page 81) Barwon Heads is located at the mouth of the Barwon River, a few kilometres downstream from its close neighbour, Ocean Grove. A craggy headland called the Bluff protects a sandy river beach, whilst just around the corner Thirteenth Beach has rolling surf along its endless stretch. Tucked behind the sand dunes of Thirteenth lies the esteemed Barwon Heads Golf Club with an 18 hole links reminiscent of the great Scottish courses.

LEFT: Pt. Lonsdale lighthouse and the infamous Rip.
RIGHT: The Bluff and river jetty at Barwon Heads.

TORQUAY AND THE SURF COAST

Torquay is a popular, bustling town that has developed dramatically over the last few years, mainly around the surfing industry and its myriad businesses, but also in its residential expansion. There are three main beaches: the more rugged back beach for surf, then the gracious and protected front beach lined with Norfolk pines, and finally Fishermans beach, which is more often than not completely becalmed. Whilst Torquay and its Surfcity Plaza are the commercial hub of the Surf Coast, its heart and soul lies at Bells Beach, just five minutes away. The Bells Beach Surfing Reserve was proclaimed by the state government in 1973, the first of its kind in the world. It is a unique location focused around the cliff-lined beach of Bells and flanked by two other breaks within the reserve: the always popular Winkipop, and Centreside. Bells' propensity for large waves has made it home to the prestigious Bells Easter Surfing Competition. This is the longest running professional surfing contest in the world and began in 1962. It's a powerful image, often seen from here, when off-shore winds and large swells give form to the ocean's energy, sweeping past in great arcs down the coast. As far back as the late 1930s, adventurous souls were surfing a variety of craft around Torquay, but it was not until the 'International Surf Carnival' of 1956 that the sport took hold. The carnival, occasioned by the Melbourne Olympics of the same year, was staged at Torquay and though it was a surf life saving event, the Californians put on an inspiring display riding their new malibu boards. Surfing's evolution became a revolution by the 1970s, spawning such legendary companies as Rip Curl and Quiksilver. However, with the advent of surfwear and corporate expansion, surfing and its alternative lifestyle became surprisingly mainstream by the 1990's.

TOP: Early morning at Winkipop, next door to Bells. BOTTOM: A becalmed and secluded bay at Point Addis. OPPOSITE: Perfect conditions at Bells Beach on sunrise.

ANGLESEA

At the foothills of the Otway Ranges, Anglesea is surrounded by bush. Just behind the town, but inconspicuous, is Alcoa's power station, fuelled by brown coal from an opencut mine nearby and supplying electricity to the smelter in Geelong. The township begins around the Anglesea River estuary and its wide grassy banks, then sprawls into the hills to be mostly consumed by the bush. The beach, though concealed from view by sand dunes, is one of the town's main attractions and continues around to Point Roadknight. This adjoining residential area with its own vast beach is protected by the slender rocky spine of Point Roadknight. As with Torquay, Ocean Grove and Lorne, Anglesea's population swells phenomenally during the summer holidays, mostly with campers injecting a good deal of colour and movement. Equally, the golf course puts on an entertaining display with its resident population of kangaroos. The putting greens can get fairly crowded, however you rarely lose a ball on this well grazed course.

In 1879 at the age of 17 years, Ernest Morrison, undertook a walk from Queenscliff to Adelaide. Extracts from his diary of the journey are reproduced in italics on the following pages. A serialized version of it appeared in a Melbourne paper entitled "Diary of a Tramp". It marked the beginning of an illustrious career as journalist and traveller, and occasional medical practitioner. In 1893 he set about on yet another epic walk covering 5,000 kilometres from Shanghai, crossing China into Burma. His account of the journey was published and resulted in his appointment as the first permanent correspondent in Asia for the London Times, based in Peking. He took up the post in 1897, staying for over 20 years, and became an expert in the politics of China. His contribution and influence was significant in the realms of international politics and earnt for him the title "Chinese Morrison".

TOP: Point Roadknight. BOTTOM: Anglesea golf course. OPPOSITE: Anglesea Beach.

AIREYS INLET

Aireys Inlet is only ten minutes away from Anglesea, with its elegant lighthouse visible most of the way. Beneath this landmark the Painkalac Creek estuary snakes around the flats below the town, but is usually sand-barred from the ocean. Aireys is surrounded by the Great Otway National Park and its heathland is regarded as one of the most significant floras in the state, boasting orchids of international renown and a blaze of colour in spring. Around the corner from Aireys is Fairhaven and its long, beautiful surf beach. At its eastern end is the Memorial Arch which marks the start of the Great Ocean Road's truly majestic journey, from here on dramatically hugging the coastline along its way. A plaque on the arch proclaims the road was built to commemorate the services of those who served in World War One. Construction of the road commenced in 1919. The section from Eastern View to Lorne was opened in 1922 and in 1932 the entire stretch between Anglesea and Apollo Bay was completed.

December 30, 1879: I left Queenscliff after an early lunch and it is my intention to endeavour to reach Bream Creek tonight, Swampy Creek tomorrow and then, by rising early and doing some hard walking, get into Lorne in time for my New Year's dinner. My attire was the subject of flattery as regards its usefulness, laughter as regards its appearance. On my head I wore a peaked hat which is certainly more suited for cold weather, but it is so made that at will I could cover all my face with it except the eyes. At Mama's earnest solicitation I got a sun shade which fits on to the cap and protects the back of the head. My clothing consisted of a thick armless woollen guernsey, my cricketing shirt and cricketing coat, serge trousers specially strengthened, comfortable socks and a light but strong pair of boots. As a protection against snakes I also wore leggings. My knapsack

LEFT: Split Point Lighthouse by moonlight. RIGHT: The Lighthouse and Painkalac Creek.

contained the following articles: 2 loaves of bread, a well roasted boneless leg of mutton, half a pound of salt, 1/4 lb. pepper, 3 lemons, 2 toothbrushes, a box of tooth powder, some rag, a towel, 5 pairs of socks, 2 cotton handkerchiefs, 2 silk, some soap and oilsilk. Writing materials and a comb, a small quotation and a note book. In the strap going round my waist was stuck a tomahawk. The only thing I carried was a billy with another one fitting inside it and this contained 4 penny boxes of matches, a box of zinc ointment, some twine, lead pencils, some flannel bandage and some calico. I was accompanied to the Barwon Heads by Harry Adams who had kindly volunteered to see me off. My knapsack was very heavy and hurt my back dreadfully. A fisherman put me across the river and I land at the Sheep Wash. I feel as I set off for Bream Creek [Breamlea] what an arduous walk I have undertaken, but with God's help I hope to get there all right. I am directed to a high sand cliff in the distance which I am told overlooks Bream Creek...

TOP LEFT: Lorne Beach. TOP RIGHT: Lorne Point. BOTTOM LEFT: Split Point Lighthouse, Aireys Inlet. BOTTOM RIGHT: Fairhaven Beach. OPPOSITE: Big Hill viewed from Cathedral Rock.

LORNE

From earliest settlement in the mid 1850s Lorne quickly became a popular tourist destination and remains one of the jewels of the Great Ocean Road, a special place of enormous charm. At the height of summer Lorne caters for an ever-changing and increasingly sophisticated holiday maker, drawn to its promenade and outdoor cafés. During the out-of-season months though, its intrinsic beauty is even more apparent, free from the summer swarms. Nestled in a protected cove, the township is enveloped by bush with an abundance of walking tracks, waterfalls and picnic grounds, most being within the Great Otway National Park. The park's most striking feature is its steep, timbered slopes to the water's edge and it is these in particular that originally gave the Great Ocean Road its reputation as one of the finest scenic routes in the world. On February 16th, 1983 the fires of Ash Wednesday desolated a large part of the park from Lorne through to Anglesea, destroying 633 houses. Today, little evidence remains of the disaster and fortunately the flora and fauna of the park have made a remarkable recovery.

LEFT: Erskine Falls. OPPOSITE: Lorne and Loutit Bay.

THE OTWAY RANGES

The Otway Ranges begin behind Anglesea and extend some one hundred kilometres, parallel to the coastline, as far as Moonlight Head. The highest peak is Mount Cowley, behind Lorne, at 634 metres. It is at the water's edge though, that the Otways are most accessible to the visitor and present a dramatic meeting of forest and ocean. Some of the best scenic views are between Lorne and Apollo Bay, where the Great Ocean Road clings to the coastline in a breathtaking manner. Having the highest rainfall in the state (over 2000mm near Lavers Hill), the Otways have an abundance of rivers and creeks flowing to the coast, most of which prompted settlement in the early days. Further Inland these meandering streams have created a wealth of waterfalls and cascades of remarkable beauty. The Otways, with its rich volcanic soil and high rainfall, are correctly described as cool temperate rainforest. One of the best places to observe the forest in all its luxuriance is Maits Rest, inland from Apollo Bay. It is a walking track which wanders through a veritable sea of tree ferns, with moss clinging to everything in a seemingly saturated environment. Some ancient myrtle beeches have developed extraordinary forms, whilst every now and again a mountain ash of monumental scale soars out of sight. Another place to penetrate the forest with ease, is Melba Gully, a beautiful picnic spot and forest walk famous for its glow-worms. The walk passes through a gully of dense forest, with an understorey of tree ferns and mosses. Nearby is the township of Lavers Hill. It straddles a high ridge along which the Great Ocean Road follows in its detour from the coast. Some of the most impressive waterfalls in the Otways are close by, including Triplet Falls, and near these falls is the Otway Fly Treetop Walk. It is a 600 metre long, 25 metre high, elevated canopy walk allowing a unique appreciation of the surrounding forest.

LEFT: Cascades below Triplet Falls. OPPOSITE: The Otway Ranges near Wye River.

A pleasant walk of 4 miles along the hard sand brought me to two deserted fishermen's huts. From a well near I got excellent water. By taking a line cross country I saved 2 miles in getting to Spring Creek [Torquay]. No less than 6 tents were pitched in a bend of the river. Spring Creek though larger than Bream and just as salt, has its mouth always barred. High tide prevented me walking round the beach to Swampy Creek [Anglesea] so I had to take to the cliffs. After having something to eat and boiling a billy of water I started. The cliffs here are magnificent. I have to walk along the edge and 300 ft below me the sea curled round the rocks or dashed against its feet... I was much struck with the cliffs passed en route. Some would be rough and ragged of a yellow colour with no trees near them, others perfectly perpendicular with the lines of formation horizontal, perpendicular or vertical. In other places cliff would rise above cliff, bare before me, but wooded on their summit, till they seemed almost to reach the sky... When boiling my billy at Swampy Creek two young residents in a house near came down to see me and their interest evinced itself more practically in the shape of a lent blanket, overcoat and pillow. My bed was in a clump of trees on the river's banks and lying awake with strange noises going on all round me I saw the Old Year 1879 out and the New Year 1880 in. In the morning when I get up half an hour before sunrise, I find I am wet through, my boots and leggings especially are soaking. My feet also are raw and in no fit state do I feel for a long walk. From the top of the hill overlooking Swampy Creek I get a most glorious view. Away to the left stretched ranges of beautiful wooded hills and as the mist still hung over the valleys it looked as if a snowy lake nestled in snug places among the hills. At the foot of the hill I am on lies Swampy Creek, placid in its smoothness and away beyond it I see the coast and cliffs

LEFT: The Upper Cumberland River, deep in the Great Otway National Park near Lorne. RIGHT: The Great Ocean Road between Lorne and Wye River on dusk.

extending miles upon miles. To my right lies the sea bank. Behind me tower still higher hills. I resolved instead of taking the ordinary road to Ayrey's Inlet through the ranges to try the old track which keeps near the coast. I start and am led by the road a most delightful walk. The sea is in sight all the time and as the coast bends round a great deal I am enabled to distinguish Eaglehawk Peak and Loutit Bay. The latter place gets more and more distinct till I can see the houses and fancy I distinguish the new hotel at the Point. Ayrey's Inlet is not a bay formed by the sea, though it may have been once. The inlet is a plain of low lying country covered with dead timber on one half, but cultivated in the half next the sea coast. Serpentining through it in an extraordinary manner is Ayrey's Inlet Creek. A large gap in the coast hills has been made by nature to enable the river to enter the sea, but for reasons best known to itself it has failed to take advantage of this. I am very thirsty. It is now 8 a.m. There is a creek 5 miles round the beach. I hurry there have a billy of tea, then going round a little further I take to the hills and follow the telegraph line

FAR LEFT: The Otway Fly's 50 metre high lookout.
LEFT: Koalas at Cape Otway. RIGHT: Hopetoun Falls.

APOLLO BAY

Apollo Bay has an impressive history of adapting to a changing world, no doubt a measure of its considerable resources and qualities. It began as a humble whaling station in 1840, sealers having frequented the area since the early 1800s. (Captain Loutit gave the town its name after his ship the Apollo took shelter in the bay.) Extensive logging commenced in the 1850s and was in turn replaced by farming in the 1880s. These past enterprises have stripped away a lot of the surrounding bush, creating a broad sweep of pasture from the Otway foothills right down to the beach. The fishing industry began in the early 1900s and although it continues today, especially in the lucrative area of crayfishing, tourism is currently the town's economic mainstay. The wide attractive foreshore is an ideal venue for regular Saturday markets and an impressive music festival staged in April. After Apollo Bay the Great Ocean Road takes to the hills and but for a glimpse of the sea at Glenaire it does not return to the coast until Princetown.

over the tops of the hills till I again descend. A wash in the Reedy Creek and I start for Lorne which I reach by 3.30. Mountjoy's is very full. In the evening I go up to the Pacific Hotel to see Ted Nicholls. He shows me over it. It is magnificently furnished equal to anything I have ever seen. After New Year's dinner I resolve to sleep out. Mrs. Mountjoy lent me blanket, mattress and pillow, Mr. Gerrard a waterproof. I spend an enjoyable night in the bathing house. Next morning after breakfast I start for Apollo Bay... After tiresome jumping over rocks I arrive at the Cumberland having passed the St. George and Sheoak. Arduous climbing for 4 miles took me to Jamieson's River – a creek very similar to the Cumberland and in a most picturesque situation. The whole of this stage was round

TOP LEFT: Apollo Bay Harbour. BOTTOM LEFT: Horse trail rides along the very long Apollo Bay Beach. OPPOSITE: Apollo Bay at the foothills of the Otway Ranges.

CAPE OTWAY

Located at the southernmost point along the Great Ocean Road, Cape Otway is best known for its historic lighthouse, completed in 1848, making it the second oldest lighthouse in Australia. Cape Otway, the first Australian landfall for sailing ships from England, and King Island mark the western entrance to Bass Strait. By navigating this fetch of water, rather than going round Tasmania, sea passage from England was reduced by a week. However, short cuts invariably come at a cost and during the early 1800s many ships were wrecked on Bass Strait's perilous reefs, with the loss of hundreds of lives. This prompted construction of the lighthouse in 1846, no easy feat considering the area was still unexplored. Within the compound is a weather station, the old telegraph station (now a museum) and the original light-keeper's quarters which have been refurbished for tourist accommodation. The lighthouse has been redundant since 1994 when a solar-powered beacon took over, but at least visitors are now permitted to ascend the lighthouse tower and marvel at the beauty and precision of its engineering. The lantern in particular is of fascinating complexity. It comprises twenty-one parabolic glass reflectors, and each of these originally had its own lamp that burned sperm-whale oil. A few kilometres before Cape Otway is a turnoff which leads to the exceptionally beautiful Blanket Bay, wonderfully isolated and protected from the westerly weather. Historically, it served as the safe landing point for provisions to the Cape Otway lighthouse, however, the supply vessels were displaced by railway and bullock wagons in the early 1900s. Today, Blanket Bay is a popular picnic and camping ground in the Great Otway National Park. There are sandy beaches with reefs for fossicking and endless rock pools for inquisitive young minds.

TOP LEFT: Blanket Bay aglow at dawn. BOTTOM LEFT: Cape Volney viewed from the top of the Cape Otway lighthouse. OPPOSITE: Cape Otway Lighthouse on dusk.

the base of huge Mt. Defiance and I thought what a happy name it had. Another rest at the *Jamieson* and then a quiet walk (though hard on my sore feet) brought me to the *Wye*. This is a remarkably picturesque river, having rising from its banks towering and splendidly wooded hills. January 3rd: Here I found camped two men, Philip Henderson and Bob Straw, who had started from Lorne 3 hours before me. As it was very late in the day and I was very leg-weary I resolved to camp and go to Apollo Bay tomorrow with them. We fitted up a *miamia*, lit a glorious fire and I slept like a top, the others found it too cold. During the night we heard the lowing of wild bulls, the howling of wild dogs and the braying of native bears. We lit a glorious fire in front of our sleeping place and at 1.45 we got up, got warm and got back to bed again. We started for Apollo Bay about half past seven. Four miles uninteresting walking over the hard but smooth rocks brought us to the *Kennet*, a fine large creek, but unfortunately salt and full of kelp. Henderson tried his hand at fishing, but unsuccessfully… After one continuous climb for an hour or so [Cape Paton] one of my companions thought that we had come to a track which we should take to the left. Accordingly we left the telegraph line and worked our way through thick scrub to the sea cliffs and we forced our way round there till we came onto the proper track, which we ought to have taken. This narrow path took us down and up delightful hills and across beautiful little fern tree gullies. Eventually we emerged into the open, having gradually descended down the narrow hills at the mouth of a creek. Here we camped for dinner. We now knew that we were only 10 miles from Apollo Bay, so started off joyfully to walk it. It was certainly the longest 10 miles I ever walked in my life and took us 5 hours exclusive of stoppages. We walked today 23 miles. We passed

LEFT: Aerial view of Cape Otway Lightstation including the old Telegraph Signal Station.
OPPOSITE: Cape Otway lighthouse viewed from the beach at Point Franklin on dusk.

13 creeks of fresh water and at each creek the scenery was more beautiful than at the others. The hills, though always very similar in their appearance never tire the eye nor become monotonous... The name Apollo, though properly applied to the bay, has been transferred to the township. It consists of one house and a pigstye, it is situated on a grassy flat fronting the sea and protected by hills... Stopping at Cawood's are two gentlemen who are on an excursion something like mine, only a pleasure one. They are Kermot and Gregory, two celebrated men; one a lecturer on Civil Engineering at the Melbourne University, the latter on Common Law. I had a glorious tea. My companions are going to stop here and tomorrow I shall go on with Kermot and Gregory as far as the Parker at least. After many delays in saddling the pack horse etc., we set off. See us on the road: Mr. Gregory, a short broad-shouldered man with a long beard, slight stoop and handsome face, wearing a helmet hat, the very type of an explorer, leading. Myself in full war paint with bare arms next and Mr. Kermot, fairly tall, with a very round back, concave breast, narrow shoulders, knock knees, red nose and spectacles leading a packhorse. This horse is a perfect wonder of a traveller. He has climbed hills whereon the foot of horse has never before alighted, he has jumped over rocks never before seen by horse's eyes and what is more wonderful has turned somersaults down hill without hurting either himself or pack. These two travellers do not much believe in roughing it. In the pack which consists of 4 large bags of canvas they carry every luxury from a tent to lime juice, sweet biscuits and figs. Our route took an upward turn for miles and miles then into the ranges for miles and miles then out again for miles and miles and following along we came into sight of the sea at Blanket Bay. Previously to this on the top of a high hill I spied a snake. In deliberating

TOP: Lush diary pasture and forest near Lavers Hill. BOTTOM: Hills near Apollo Bay. OPPOSITE: Anchors from the "Marie Gabrielle" on Wreck Beach at Moonlight Head.

ABOVE: Rolling hills of the Otways near Lavers Hill. OPPOSITE: Summer storm over the Twelve Apostles Marine National Park at Clifton Beach.

ABOVE: Looking towards Moonlight Head across Gibson Steps Beach. OPPOSITE: Aerial view of the Twelve Apostles and the hinterland.

The Gellibrand River at Princetown marks the beginning of the Port Campbell National Park which stretches 27 kilometres to Peterborough, mostly as a narrow strip of coastal heathland lying between the Great Ocean Road and the sea. The park is famous not so much for its flora and fauna, but its dramatic and intricate coastline, depicted so dynamically by the Twelve Apostles. The limestone cliffs began to form 10-20 million years ago under the sea from the buildup of skeletons of minute marine animals. Yet, it is only relatively recently that the erosion visible today commenced, due to changing sea-levels 5,000-7,000 years ago. The rock stacks are formed by the gradual erosion of softer limestone, forming caves into the cliffs. If they are on a headland, these caves eventually become arches and when they collapse a rock island is left detached. The cliffs rise to nearly 70 metres in places and the highest Apostle is about 45 metres. On the beach below the viewing platform is a colony of fairy penguins.

how we were to kill it, it slipped into a log and we were delayed half an hour getting it much to Mr. Kermot's disgust. It was only by luck we did dislodge it after all. I could clearly see disappointment in the physiognomy of its countenance as it spat, jumped and got killed at the same moment. Imagine the poor thing's feelings, whilst laughing in its sleeve at our hacks at the wrong limb, to be suddenly disturbed by a pointed stick. If it had kept quiet it would even then have been safe, but it so boiled over with indignation that it couldn't hold itself and came out. A whack with a stick ended the fun. From Blanket Bay we kept a well beaten dray path to the Parker, a beautiful river with rustic bridge. Here I left my companions and went on alone. On rounding a hill I saw what looked like a church on the top of a hill. I made my way to this and was welcomed in most hospitably

LEFT: Rock stack at Gibson Steps Beach. OPPOSITE: The Twelve Apostles from a boat.

by Kelsall, the telegraph operator. He was most cordial, gave me a good tea and a shakedown on the sofa. Next day, Monday, in the morning I was shown round. Visited the caves and limestone grottoes and went up the lighthouse. The man in charge showed us the revolving apparatus. The light is called a revolving light of the first order, transmitting a flash once every minute. There are 21 lamps and it takes 7 lamps to make a flash, so it will be perceived the whole affair turns round in 3 minutes. The lighthouse is very short and stumpy looking, but this gives additional strength. The walls are 5 ft. thick and the tower is round. The only residents on the Cape which is the southernmost part of Australia are those who have to be there in an official capacity such as the telegraph operator, the man in charge of the lighthouse and his assistants. On taking leave of Kelsall I of course asked him what the bill was. He seemed quite annoyed at my doing so and asked me what I should think of a man who expected to be paid for a night's board and lodging by the only stranger he had seen for 6 months. His last few words raised my respect for him... January 6th: That night I slept like a top. The next morning at 7.30 I started. Jim Anderson said I would see a track going up a hill and I was to follow that to Princetown. Over the hills to the river Johanna, previous to which I had crossed a small creek and once beyond the Johanna and up a sand hill or two I got on to the track. It was just a narrow footpath 18 inches wide and I couldn't expect it to be very clearly defined, as it had only once been crossed within the preceding 12 months. It first kept along the edge of the cliffs, but gradually edging off to my astonishment it struck clean away into the forest, apparently on the top of a dividing range. After walking 12 miles or so in this direction without hardly seeing the sun, the foliage became so dense as to completely cover

TOP & BOTTOM: The Twelve Apostles before and after the collapse of one of the rock stacks in 2005. OPPOSITE: The Twelve Apostles, glorious at sunset (pre 2005).

LOCH ARD GORGE

Loch Ard Gorge is famous for the wreck of the Loch Ard, a three-masted clipper that went down with the loss of 52 lives. A walk recounting the tragic story takes you from the wreck site to the cemetery then onto the beach below, enclosed by cliffs. It is one of many themed walks, within the sizable Loch Ard precinct, that link the various attractions and explain the geology of the coastline. At dusk each night between September and May thousands of Muttonbirds can be seen returning to their nests on Muttonbird Island, swooping and circling in an almost frenzied state. Correctly known as the Short-tailed Shearwater, it was given its name by the early settlers for its fatty, mutton-flavoured flesh. Each year it undertakes a remarkable 30,000 kilometre migration around the Pacific Ocean. The journey starts in mid April and it takes them two months to reach their wintering grounds around the Aleutian Islands, below Alaska and Siberia. They return by continuing to circle the Pacific, following the prevailing winds down North America's coast and arrive home with uncanny regularity on or about the 22nd of September. It was a reef extending from Muttonbird Island onto which the Loch Ard was swept during the early hours of June 1st, 1878. The ship went down within 15 minutes and Eva Carmichael and Tom Pearce, the only two survivors, were washed into the gorge and eventually rescued. (See page 88) To visit Loch Ard Gorge with a large ground swell running, is to observe the full force of the ocean's might at close quarters (and better comprehend the plight of the Loch Ard). Giant waves crashing onto cliffs with spectacular effects abound, but Broken Head offers the best experience, especially backlit by the late afternoon's sun. It is at the western end of the precinct and overlooks massive waves in their amazing beauty.

TOP: Island Arch. BOTTOM: One of the caves at Loch Ard Gorge. OPPOSITE: Aerial view of the Loch Ard Gorge precinct with Muttonbird Island in the foreground.

the path, all of a sudden as it seemed to me, it turned gradually round and made for the coast through forest characterized by larger trees, but not such a dense undergrowth. This made the track harder to distinguish than before and often when it branched into 2 or 3 narrow paths I was in dread lest I should take a wrong turning and get off the proper road. I never once hesitated, but always went straight ahead and to this fact I owe my getting to the Gellibrand that night. I feel now what a dangerous walk it was, in fact it almost makes me shudder to think how easily I could have left the path for maybe death... The total distance I had walked today was 35 miles. Next morning, Wednesday, I didn't get up till late I was so tired and after breakfast talked with a young lady, a Miss Jessie Curdie, 3rd daughter of Dr. Curdie of Tandarook, till dinner time. She is 5 feet 4, 8 stone 6, with a good figure, pleasing face, nice voice and most fascinating manners. Mrs. Gibson is very kind. The house [Glenample Homestead] is a stone one and is situated on the sea side of a hill sloping upwards to the sea bank. The front view takes in the view of the

LEFT: Loch Ard Gorge. OPPOSITE: A large swell viewed from Broken Head across Sherbrook River.

country as far as the eye can reach towards Camperdown etc. In the afternoon went down on to the beach with Miss Curdie. Mr Gibson had cut in the perpendicular face of the cliff stone steps leading down to the beach and also has had excavated a famous tunnel cut through solid rock of a headland to make accessible another stretch of beach beyond. The cliffs all about here and for miles round are perfectly perpendicular, at places having immense gorges also with perpendicular sides running into the land and nearly always washed by the sea waves. The most peculiar characteristic, however, is the number of immense rocks or rather detached cliffs standing away from the land and surrounded with reefs all about the coast. Many of these must be the size of a large church and of course have never been climbed [12 Apostles]... The gorge into which Tom Pearce and Miss Carmichael were washed is about 150 yards to the right, that is the west of where the Loch Ard struck. The Gorge running in first has a narrow opening which gradually widens till it is met by a headland running out from the land which divides it into two other gorges. The celebrated cave however, is just round the first corner to the west arriving in from the sea. It runs straight out in the direction of the sea for a distance of 75 yards. The beach is accessible only by means of steps cut down the headland into the west gorge and it was at the extremity of the headland, also on the west that Tom Pearce scaled. The caves are very pretty, of lime formation, water dripping through the ceiling having formed pretty little stalactites. They are very cold and are said to be the home of bats. The smaller gorges are covered with wreckage and a fine spar was on the beach... [January 15th] Port Campbell I come upon quite unexpectedly. I could see before I ascended the final hill houses away up a river, but I didn't know till came down the hill and came upon a large house, evidently

TOP: Glenample Homestead. BOTTOM: The Gellibrand River below Princetown. OPPOSITE: A heavy sea viewed from Broken Head at Loch Ard Gorge at sunset.

Just on sunset, the Discovery Walk along the cliff of Port Campbell Bay often reveals the striking form of Sentinel Rock and surrounding cliffs bathed in extraordinary hues. Adding to the display is the constant pounding by waves producing dramatic explosions of spray. Yet in the midst of this wildly exposed area is a remarkably protected inlet, around which is nestled the small township of Port Campbell. This picturesque bay, lined with Norfolk Pines, has a small sandy beach and a jetty which serves as the launching place for the local crayfishing fleet. Port Campbell was settled in the 1870s and came to prominence in 1878 with the wreck of the Loch Ard and subsequent salvage operations that were organized from the town. The 98 ton paddle steamer 'Napier' was chartered to access the wreck, however, it too was wrecked opposite the jetty, during heavy seas. Some years after the Loch Ard tragedy a rocket shed was constructed near the jetty for the purpose of shipwreck rescue. It was replaced in the 1930s and now houses a display which explains how a small rocket was used

LEFT: Moonrise over Port Campbell National Park.
RIGHT: Port Campbell and its dairying hinterland.

to propel carefully coiled lines across the water to those stranded aboard ship. As road and rail links developed so did the town and by the 1890s it was emerging as a holiday resort with several guest houses. They have long ago been replaced by motels and slowly the unsophisticated charm of the town is disappearing. Hopefully its natural beauty and surrounding wonders will survive the relentless and sometimes inappropriate demands of tourism. For a while it looked like there might be more than rock stacks to gaze upon out to sea, when significant gas reserves were found offshore in the Otway Basin. (For years inland gas wells have supplied local towns.) Exploration was originally aimed at finding oil as in Eastern Bass Strait, but so far its only gas. Today BHP, Santos and Woodside are all extracting this gas from separate fields using subsea wells and $700 million have been spent on infrastructure including three processing plants at locations each about six kilometres from Port Campbell.

a store, that the bay I saw was Port Campbell and the creek was Campbell's Creek. The scenery about was a great change from the everlasting bald prospect. The bay is broad and deep and runs in a good distance. The water in it is very deep and there is excellent anchorage. It is not however a safe port, being too much exposed to the south and S.W. winds and there is also some difficulty in getting into it, owing to a reef of rocks which runs out from the east extremity to a distance of a mile. The bay is brought to a standstill by a low sea bank, though the valley of the creek, a valley about as broad as the port itself runs away between high hills as far as you can see. On the W. shore is the wreck of the Napier and one of its boats is lying on the beach... Walking along every now and then you catch

TOP: Port Campbell jetty. BOTTOM: Port Campbell's rugged backdrop. OPPOSITE: Sentinel Rock on dusk viewed from the Discovery Walk alongside Port Campbell Bay.

THE ARCH AND LONDON BRIDGE

The timeless pounding of waves has altered the shape of many once famous formations in the Port Campbell National Park. The slender main arch of London Bridge collapsed in 1990, however the remaining arch presents a fine structure and visitors' imaginations do the rest. London Bridge's other and more resilient attraction is that of the Fairy or Little Penguin which nests on the beach, protected by surrounding cliffs. As with most flightless birds, the Fairy Penguin is a beguiling oddity and by quirk of nature it seems to think it's a fish. It is the smallest penguin species, found only in Southern Australia and New Zealand. Their colonies vary in size from a few dozen birds to thousands and they live in burrows 60-80 centimetres long, dug out laboriously with their feet. The breeding season is between May and October and this is when most birds are found ashore during the day. Two eggs are laid and brooded by both parents until at about two months the fledgling takes on its daily life at sea. This begins before dawn and ends after dark when the penguins straggle ashore in small groups. Their mobility on land is not much better than their

LEFT: The Arch. OPPOSITE: London Bridge nearby.

a glimpse of the inhospitable coast. Always the water washed cliffs, with the huge detached rocks and sea dashing round them. I pass by the first house I come to and keep on over a sandy road till I come to a large house standing among a lot of ferns. I feel sure this is Irvine's and go across to see. On my telling my name he asked me in to dinner. Before doing so he took me across to show me the bay of islands. There is nothing very remarkable in this. Just an inlet studded with lofty detached cliffs. The centre one of all is called Lot's Wife. Mr. Irvine says I am uneducated because I do not go in for Poetry, Sketching and Phrenology. He shows me original specimens of the two former and they excite my admiration. He tells me he looks at everything in the humorous light and versifies after the same style as Mark Twain in the Innocents Abroad. My head is examined. I have strong moral character, never swear, teetotaller, and keen sense of the ridiculous. Have no amativeness, combativeness, but strong religious feelings. I would make a good parson or a merchant as I have a good business head, am steady and of sedentary inclinations. There is no use my trying to be a doctor as I have neither courage, energy, endurance, determination nor self esteem. Have great affection for animals no destructiveness,

complete inability to become airborne. But, they can seemingly fly underwater. Their short wings, acting as paddles, and streamlined body shape are beautifully adapted for the marine environment, enabling great speed and agility. A few kilometres west of London Bridge lies the massive Curdies Inlet, always resplendent with birdlife, and beside it the township of Peterborough. On one side of the estuary are large sand dunes and an exposed beach, whilst on the other there is a return to low sandstone cliffs carved into a complex pattern of coves and secluded beaches. It is hard to believe that on a calm, moonlit night in 1855 the Schomberg, one of the largest and most luxurious clippers of the period, ran aground 200 metres offshore on her maiden voyage. Fortunately no lives were lost, but the reputation of the Schomberg's captain, "Bully" Forbes, was lost from then on. Peterborough is a popular haven for Victoria's western-district farmers, many of whom frequent the Peterborough Golf Club. This golf course suits golfers of all abilities, given its forgiving nature and despite being located, at times, a bit too close to the ocean.

LEFT: The Bay of Islands. RIGHT: The Bay of Martyrs.

am remarkably good-tempered and never subject to obstinacy... I wasn't long now getting on to the mainroad and as it was very late hurried on like the mischief. After walking 2 miles I got into Portland and stopped at the first hotel I met. I was too tired to eat anything, so asked for my room. Some distance had to be gone over uncarpeted stairs and balcony till I got to it. The flies were frightful, the room smelt horribly. I threw open the window as high as it would go and jumped into one of the beds. There were two others in the room. The fleas were in countless numbers. In the morning I wasn't called till breakfast was finished, so all I got was some cold fish recooked, old bread and rancid butter. My bill came to 2 shillings and sixpence. Perhaps it will be as well to remember the name of the house of dirt. It was the 'Lamb' hotel owned by a S. McConachy, late of Geelong who told me he was a friend of my father's. I strolled about before leaving. Portland is a flourishing place and is connected by railway with Melbourne. The bay especially is very fine and there is a long new wharf situated between the old wharf and a tumbledown bathing house... I was accosted by a military looking fellow, who asked me one or two questions. I told him who I was and what I was travelling for. He immediately became very friendly and without the slightest reserve told me that he was the State School teacher and had done trips similar to mine for many years in New Zealand. He introduced me to a squatter from the Wimmera stopping here, a Mr. Wettenhall, a short sturdy looking little fellow with a very pleasing face. His manner of introduction was characteristic "Mr. Wettenhall this is Mr. Morrison who to my mind is doing a very plucky thing. He has walked all the way from Queenscliff round the coast and intends to go on to Adelaide. What makes it all the more plucky is that he is 17 years of age and has never done anything like it before."

TOP: Aerial of Peterborough surrounded by golf course and the Curdies River estuary. BOTTOM: Peterborough's main beach. OPPOSITE: Rock stacks at the Bay of Islands.

WARRNAMBOOL

Warrnambool is one of the main trading centres for Victoria's rural western district and has a population of about 30,000, which makes it the largest city on the Great Ocean Road. It's a bustling, sophisticated city that sustains a large retail shopping sector and diverse cultural and sporting facilities, yet possesses a strong coastal flavour that is most engaging. Numerous avenues of old Norfolk pines also make for a very attractive city. Lady Bay provides the focus for many recreational and tourist attractions including protected beaches, Lake Pertobe adventure playground and the Flagstaff Hill Maritime Museum. It is here at the museum that Warrnambool's early history as a busy coastal port is re-created. The spirit and heritage of the coastline are captured by the museum's collection of historic ships, buildings, nautical displays and sound and laser presentation. It also includes a detailed account of the once thriving whaling industry in the area. These days, though, the focus has shifted to that of nurturing whales, in particular at the protected whale nursery at Logans beach. It was a very different story 160 years ago, though. The blubber of an average Southern Right Whale (15 metres long and weighing 50 tonnes), produced up to 8,500 litres of oil when boiled down in the traditional 'trypots'. It was a high quality industrial oil with many applications including mechanical lubrication and cosmetics. Hunting of these docile creatures was relatively easy because they swam slowly and very close to the shore, and by the 1890s they were almost extinct. The worldwide population is now estimated to be around 2,000 and every May, female Southern Right Whales come to Warrnambool to calve. They can be easily seen close to the shore over several months before they depart in October for their Antarctic summer feeding grounds.

TOP LEFT: Southern Right Whale at Logans Beach. (photograph D. Parer, Auscape).
BOTTOM LEFT & OPPOSITE: Historic buildings at Flagstaff Hill Maritime Museum.

PORT FAIRY

Steeped in history and charm, Port Fairy is located at the mouth of the Moyne River which provides a natural harbour, flurried with yachts and fishing boats. The hunting of whales and seals in the past has given way to crayfish and abalone fishing as is appropriate for a town with a reputation for fine food and sumptuous accommodation. The whalers' and sealers' contact with the area dates back to the early 1800s, but it was not until 1843 that two Irish land developers surveyed and subdivided the township naming it Belfast, though the harbour was always known as Port Fairy. Fellow Irish folk needed little encouragement to emigrate and escape the potato famine blighting their homeland. In celebration of this strong Irish heritage, Port Fairy hosts Australia's largest folk music festival each year in March. The town's colourful history has produced a wealth of historic buildings, mostly constructed in the local volcanic bluestone, of which over fifty are classified by the National Trust.

Mr. Chas L. Money, the schoolmaster, is an extraordinary man. In appearance he is 5 feet 11 inches high, broad shouldered and remarkably well made. He has fair hair, blue eyes an energetic nose and determined mouth. He is of a very impetuous disposition, very impatient of rebuke. He is 40 years of age, but being so fashionably dressed and wearing such a handsome moustache easily might be mistaken for 25... He has been several things in Victoria, was at the diggings, was a swagman and at another time was a traveller for a photographer. Nine years ago he received a situation at the Geelong Grammar School. He got drunk and was dismissed. He has been a teetotaller since, is now earning £100 a year as a State School teacher and is engaged to be married to a girl who subscribes herself in her letters 'Your loving little kitten.' Not withstanding Mr. McKinley

TOP: 'Talara' built in 1854. BOTTOM: Tower Hill. OPPOSITE: Moyne River at Port Fairy.

PORTLAND

Portland Bay was one of the best whale areas in the world with annual catches running into hundreds during the early 1800s. However, it was not until 1834 that farming prospects encouraged the Henty brothers from Tasmania to till the soil, thereby establishing Portland as the first European settlement in Victoria. The city today revolves around its deep-water shipping port which sustains a broad range of industries, the largest of which is the aluminium smelter. Portland is also noteworthy for its geothermal energy program, using 60°C water from bores 1200 metres deep. To the west of Portland is Cape Bridgewater. On the eastern side of the cape is the small and protected township, whilst on the more exposed side are the legendary Blowholes. A large swell pounding against the dramatic black volcanic rock remains a spectacular and captivating display of the elements. Close by, and a picture of serenity by comparison, are the extraordinary sand dunes of the Discovery Bay Coastal Park.

professed his inability to make me comfortable, I could not have been more so. In the morning before breakfast we men had a bathe in the sea. The breakers were glorious and it was very enjoyable. Cape Bridgewater is the western extremity of deep bay, the other cape opposite being Cape Nelson. McKinley's house is situated on the slope of this high headland, looking towards Cape Nelson. Below is a rocky beach, but at the head of the bay is a long strip of beautiful sand. The bay is the finest I have ever seen. It is protected by high hills, the majority of which are covered with the usual vegetation seen near the sea, but there is one strip about a mile long on the E. side of the bay of perfectly white sand mountains... [January 22nd] In the afternoon I went much further round the coast to see some blowholes. Nothing I have seen anywhere round the coast can be even compared

TOP: Portland Bay. BOTTOM: Cape Nelson Lighthouse. OPPOSITE: The Blowholes.

CAPE BRIDGEWATER

with the sublime scenery thereof. It was a calm day when I saw it, yet often when the waves struck the rocks they would send up a cloud of spray far above our heads and we were sitting eighty feet above the water on a ledge of rock. The cliffs here are of a dark blue colour, in formation and general appearance something like the pictures of the Giant's Causeway. On a rough day you cannot come near the top of the cliffs at all or you would be wet through instantly. We saw two blowholes. Immediately after a wave thunders up against the rocks a huge puff of steam, smoke or water or something or other, shoots out of these holes with a noise like a cannon. The rougher the weather, the louder the explosion. The waves are sublime they are magnificent. By Jerusalem I wish I could describe them. I know I could have looked at them for hours without getting tired. Mr. Money can't go near the edge of the cliffs, as he is seized with an irresistible desire to throw himself in and several times it has been all he could do to prevent himself.

TOP LEFT: Cape Bridgewater and dramatic seacliffs. TOP RIGHT & OPPOSITE: Discovery Bay Coastal Park sand dunes. BOTTOM LEFT: Petrified Forest near Cape Bridgewater. BOTTOM RIGHT: Fur seal.

Queenscliff
- Population 1,500
- Queenscliff Music Festival in November

Marine Discovery Centre (03 5258 3344)
Maritime Museum
Fort Queenscliff Museum
Organized heritage walks
Queenscliff Historical Centre
Bellarine Peninsula Steam Railway
Wharf and ferry services across Port Phillip Bay
Lighthouses (only bluestone lighthouse in Australia)
Swan Bay and birdlife
Community Market

Point Lonsdale
- Population 2,000

Lighthouse and Jetty below
Views of the Rip and ships passing through
Front beach promenade and ocean beach
Community market

Ocean Grove
- Population 12,000

Lake Connewarre and birdlife
Wirruna Nursery and gardens at Wallington
Protected ocean beach

Barwon Heads
- Population 3,200

Barwon River estuary and prolific birdlife
The Bluff limestone headland

Barwon Heads cont.
Golf Courses
Jirrahlinga Koala & Wildlife Sanctuary
Thirteenth Beach especially for surfing

Torquay
- Population 10,000
- Bells Beach Rip Curl Pro Surfing Competition at Easter
- High Tide Festival (community arts & culture) in Dec.

Bells Beach Surfing Recreation Reserve
Surfworld Museum
Surfcity Plaza retail centre for surfgear and surfwear
Variety of beaches for surfing and also safe swimming

Anglesea
- Population 2,200

Anglesea Golf Course and resident kangaroos
River Estuary and Coogoorah Park wetlands
Native Orchids in the Bald Hills area during spring
Point Roadknight headland and protected beach
Tours around Alcoa Power Station (03 5263 4249)

Aireys Inlet
- Population 1,000

Split Point Lighthouse
Great Otway National Park
Allen Noble Sanctuary for waterbirds
Distillery Creek & Moggs Creek picnic grounds
Great Ocean Road Memorial Arch at Eastern View
Native Orchids in the heathland during spring
Ocean beaches and low tide reef walks

Lorne
- Population 1,200
- Lorne Pier to Pub Swim Classic in January
- The Falls Music Festival in December

Great Otway National Park
Bushwalks and picnic grounds
Erskine Falls and many others
The bay, pier and beach
Cumberland River
Cinema (the only one on the coast till Warrnambool)
Restaurants and promenade with outdoor cafés
Historical Society
Qdos Art Gallery

Wye River
- Population 200

Great Otway National Park
Ocean beaches
Foreshore camping and caravan park

Kennett River
- Population 100

Great Otway National Park
Ocean beaches
Foreshore camping and caravan park

Skenes Creek
- Population 300

Great Otway National Park
Ocean beaches
Foreshore camping and caravan park

Apollo Bay

- Population 1,200
- Apollo Bay Music Festival in April
- The Great Ocean Road International Marathon in May

Great Otway National Park

Marriners Falls

Maits Rest rainforest walk

Fishing harbour and Fisherman's Co-Op

Historical Museum or "Old Cable Station Museum"

Marriners Lookout

Turtons Track forest drive

Cape Otway Lighthouse (20 minute drive)

Foreshore community market every Saturday morning

Lavers Hill

- Population 300

Great Otway National Park

Triplet, Hopetoun & Beauchamp waterfalls

The Otway Fly Treetop Walk (03 5235 9200)

Melba Gully rainforest walk

Tearooms

Princetown

- Population 100

Port Campbell National Park

Gellibrand River estuary and birdlife

Glenample Homestead and historic displays

Port Campbell

- Population 350

Port Campbell Bay with jetty and safe beach

Port Campbell cont.

Port Campbell National Park (including the Twelve Apostles, Loch Ard Gorge & London Bridge)

Discovery Walk to Two Mile Bay

Historical Society

Timboon Farmhouse Cheese (biodynamic cheeses)

Peterborough

- Population 250

Port Campbell National Park

Bay of Martyrs and Bay of Islands and their rock stacks

Curdies River estuary and abundant birdlife

Peterborough golf links

Warrnambool

- Population 31,000
- Horse Racing Carnival and Steeplechase in May
- Fun 4 Kids Festival during June school holidays

Flagstaff Hill Maritime Museum & Sound & Laser Show

Logans Beach Southern Right Whale nursery

Warrnambool Art Gallery

Lake Pertobe adventure playground

Lady Bay foreshore promenade

Tower Hill State Game Reserve

Botanic Gardens designed by William Guilfoyle

Port Fairy

- Population 2600
- Port Fairy Folk Music Festival (Labour Day weekend)
- Port Fairy Spring Music Festival in October

Boat harbour on the Moyne River

Port Fairy cont.

Griffiths Island Lighthouse and muttonbird colony

Historic Buildings (including Motts Cottage)

Lady Julia Percy Island seal colony and birdlife

Port Fairy History Centre

The Crags rugged coastline lookout

Mount Eccles National Park

Codrington wind farm

Protected ocean beach

Portland

- Population 10,000

Maritime Discovery Centre

Botanic Gardens and historic cottage

Burswood Homestead Gardens

Historic buildings and History House Museum

Cape Nelson Lighthouse & State Park

Harbour and wharves accessible to the public

Tours around Portland Aluminium Smelter

Powerhouse Motor and Car Museum

Gannet colony at Point Danger

Protected ocean beach

Cape Bridgewater

- Population 100

Bridgewater Bay and massive seacliffs

The Blowholes

Petrified Forest geological formation

Discovery Bay Coastal Park and sand dunes

Seal colony and attendant boat tours

[Refer also to internet sites on pages 64 & 72]

VISITOR INFORMATION CENTRES

Queenscliff
Queenscliff Visitor Information Centre
55 Hesse Street, Queenscliff
Tel. 1300 884 843 or 03 5258 4843
www.queenscliff.org

Torquay
Torquay Visitor Information Centre
Surfcity Plaza, Torquay
Tel: 1300 614 219 or 03 5261 4219
www.visitsurfcoast.com

Lorne
Lorne Visitor Information Centre
15 Mountjoy Parade, Lorne
Tel. 1300 891 152 or 03 5289 1152
www.visitsurfcoast.com

Apollo Bay
Great Ocean Road Visitor Information Centre
Foreshore, Apollo Bay
Tel. 03 5237 6529
www.visitapollobay.com or www.visitotways.com

Port Campbell
Port Campbell Visitor Information Centre
26 Morris Street, Port Campbell
Tel. 1300 137 255 or 03 5598 6089
www.visit12apostles.com

Warrnambool
Warrnambool Visitor Information Centre
23 Merri Street, Warrnambool
Tel. 1800 637 725 or 03 5559 4620
www.warrnamboolinfo.com.au

Port Fairy
Port Fairy Visitor Information Centre
Bank Street, Port Fairy
Tel. 03 5568 2682
www.myportfairy.com
www.port-fairy.com

Portland
Portland Visitor Information Centre
Lee Breakwater Road (the foreshore), Portland
Tel. 1800 035 567
Tel. 03 5523 2671

Nelson
Nelson Visitor Information Centre
Leake Street, Nelson
Tel. 08 8738 4051

NATIONAL PARK & STATE PARK OFFICES

Great Otway National Park
Anglesea Office
Tel. 03 5263 4205
Lorne Office
Tel. 03 5289 4100
Forrest Work Centre
Tel. 03 5236 6204
Apollo Bay Office
Tel. 03 5237 2500
Lavers Hill Work Centre
Tel. 03 5237 3243

Port Campbell National Park
Tel. 03 5598 6382

Tower Hill State Game Reserve
Tel. 03 5565 9202

Mount Eccles National Park
Tel. 03 5576 1338

Cape Nelson State Park & Mt Richmond National Pk
Tel. 03 5522 3440

Discovery Bay Coastal Park
Tel. 08 8738 4051

Lower Glenelg National Park
Tel. 08 8738 4051

Princess Margaret Rose Caves
Tel. 08 8738 4171

Parks Victoria Information Line (24 hours)
Tel. 131963

HOSPITALS & MEDICAL CENTRES

Geelong
Geelong Hospital
272 Ryrie Street, Geelong
24 hour service:
Tel. 03 5226 7111
Tel. 03 5226 7564 for emergency

Queenscliff
Queenscliff Surgery
2 King Street, Queenscliff
Tel. 03 5258 2353

Point Lonsdale
Point Lonsdale Medical Group
Nelson Road, Point Lonsdale
Tel. 03 5258 0888

Ocean Grove
Ocean Grove Medical Centre
75 The Parade, Ocean Grove
Tel. 03 5255 1022

Barwon Heads
Barwon Heads Medical Clinic
74 Hitchcock Avenue, Barwon Heads
Tel. 03 5254 2727

Torquay
Surfcoast Medical Centre
100 Surf Coast Highway, Torquay
Tel. 03 5261 1111

Anglesea
Surfcoast Medical Centre
McMillan Street, Anglesea
Tel. 03 5263 1952

Aireys Inlet
Aireys Inlet Medical Centre
64 Great Ocean Road, Aireys Inlet
Tel. 03 5289 6432

Lorne
•Lorne Community Hospital
Albert Street, Lorne
Tel. 03 5289 4300
•Lorne Medical Centre
230 Mountjoy Parade, Lorne
Tel. 03 5289 2005

Apollo Bay
Apollo Bay & District Hospital
McLachlan Street, Apollo Bay
Tel. 03 5237 8500

Apollo Bay General Practice
40 Pascoe Street, Apollo Bay
Tel. 03 5237 6844

Port Campbell
Timboon & District Hospital
Hospital Road, Timboon
Tel. 03 5558 6000

Port Campbell cont.
Timboon Medical Clinic
14 Hospital Road, Timboon
Tel. 03 5558 6088

Warrnambool
Warrnambool Hospital
Ryot Street, Warrnambool
Tel. 03 5563 1666

Warrnambool Medical Clinic
193A Liebig Street, Warrnambool
Tel. 03 5562 2766

Port Fairy
Port Fairy Hospital
Villiers Street, Port Fairy
Tel. 03 5568 0100

Port Fairy Medical Clinic
28 Villiers Street, Port Fairy
Tel. 03 5568 1559

Portland
Portland and District Hospital
Bentinck Street, Portland
Tel. 03 5521 0333

Seaport Medical Centre
6 Fern Street, Portland
Tel. 03 5523 2322

PATROLLED BEACHES WITH SURF LIFE SAVING CLUBS

Point Lonsdale...............03 5258 1257	Anglesea...............03 5263 1617	Apollo Bay...............03 5237 6765
Ocean Grove...............03 5255 1382	Fairhaven...............03 5289 6275	Port Campbell...............03 5598 6275
Thirteenth Beach at Barwon Heads........03 5254 2469	Lorne...............03 5289 1724	Warrnambool...............03 5561 1790
Torquay...............03 5261 4110	Wye River...............03 5289 0297	Port Fairy...............03 5568 2246
Jan Juc...............03 5261 2602	Kennett River...............03 5289 0277	Cape Bridgewater near Portland...............03 5526 7233

POLICE STATIONS

Queenscliff...............03 5258 4285	Lorne...............03 5289 2712	Warrnambool...............03 5560 1333
Ocean Grove...............03 5256 2698	Apollo Bay...............03 5237 6750	Port Fairy...............03 5568 1007
Torquay...............03 5261 6058	Lavers Hill...............03 5237 3200	Portland...............03 5523 1999
Anglesea...............03 5263 3468	Port Campbell...............03 5598 6310	Emergency Attendance...............000

GOLF COURSES

Queenscliff Golf Club...............03 5258 1951	Torquay Golf Club...............03 5261 2005	Timboon Golf Club...............03 5598 3297
Point Lonsdale Golf Club...............03 5258 1955	The Sands, Torquay...............03 5264 8801	Peterborough Golf Club...............03 5598 5245
Ocean Grove Golf Club...............03 5256 2795	Anglesea Golf Club...............03 5263 1582	Warrnambool Golf Club...............03 5562 2108
Barwon Heads Golf Club...............03 5255 6255	Lorne Golf Club...............03 5289 1267	Port Fairy Golf Club...............03 5568 1654
13th Beach Golf Links, Barwon Heads....03 5254 2922	Apollo Bay Golf Club...............03 5237 6474	Portland Golf Club...............03 5523 2523

GENERAL TRAVEL INFORMATION

Airlines
Qantas...............131313
Jetstar...............131538
Virgin Blue...............136789

Railway & Buslines
V-Line Rail & Coach...............136196
Gull Airport Service...............03 5222 4966

Car Rental
Avis...............136333
Budget...............132727
Hertz...............1300 132607
Thrifty...............1300 367227

Ferry - Queenscliff to Sorrento (and vice versa)
Hourly 7am to 6pm every day...............03 5258 3244

Campervan Rental
Apollo...............1800 777779
Britz...............1800 331454
Kea...............1800 252555
Maui...............1300 363800

RACV
Emergency Road Service...............131111

TRAVELLING TIMES BETWEEN TOWNS

Geelong to Queenscliff.....................31 km....25 mins
Geelong to Torquay ....21 km.... 15 mins
Geelong to Lorne ....65 km....55 mins
Geelong to Warrnambool (H'way)... 190 km.... 2 hours
Queenscliff to Barwon Heads.................18 km.... 15 mins
Barwon Heads to Torquay ....25 km.... 18 mins

Torquay to Anglesea ....17 km.... 15 mins
Anglesea to Aireys Inlet ....10 km....08 mins
Aireys Inlet to Lorne ....18 km....20 mins
Lorne to Wye River ....17 km....20 mins
Wye River to Apollo Bay.............................30 km....25 mins
Apollo Bay to Lavers Hill.............................50 km....40 mins

Lavers Hill to Port Campbell.....................51 km....40 mins
Port Campbell to Warrnambool ....66 km....45 mins
Warrnambool to Port Fairy.....................30 km....20 mins
Port Fairy to Portland ....69 km....50 mins
Portland to Cape Bridgewater.................25 km.... 15 mins
Portland to Nelson ....66 km....45 mins

MUSEUMS & HISTORICAL SOCIETIES

Queenscliff

Queenscliff Historical Centre
Hesse Street, Queenscliff
Tel. 03 5258 2511

Queenscliff Maritime Museum
Wharf Street, Queenscliff
Tel. 03 5258 3440

Fort Queenscliff Museum
King Street, Queenscliff
Tel. 03 5258 1488 & 03 5258 3403

Torquay

Surfworld Museum
Surfcity Plaza, Torquay
Tel. 03 5261 4606

Anglesea

Anglesea Historical Society
5A McMillan Street, Anglesea
Tel. 03 5263 1249

Lorne

Lorne Historical Society
16 Mountjoy Parade, Lorne
Tel. 03 5243 1249 or 0417 517 253

Apollo Bay

Historical Museum or "Old Cable Station Museum"
Great Ocean Road, Apollo Bay
Tel. 03 5237 7441

Port Campbell

• Glenample Homestead
Great Ocean Road, near Gibson Steps Beach
Tel. 131963
• Port Campbell Historical Society
Lord Street, Port Campbell
Tel. 03 5598 6390

Warrnambool

Flagstaff Hill Maritime Museum
23 Merri Street, Warrnambool
Tel. 1800 556 111 or 03 5559 4600

Warrnambool cont.

History House
Gilles Street, Warrnambool
Tel. 03 5562 6940

Port Fairy

Port Fairy History Centre
30 Gipps Street, Port Fairy
Tel. 03 5568 2263

Portland

History House
Cliff Street, Portland
Tel. 03 5522 2266

Portland Powerhouse Vintage Car Museum
Cnr Percy & Glenelg Streets, Portland
Tel. 03 5523 5795

Portland Maritime Discovery Centre
Portland Visitor Information Centre
Tel. 03 5523 2671 or 1800 035 567

ART GALLERIES

Queenscliff
Seaview Gallery
86 Hesse Street, Queenscliff
Tel. 03 5258 3645

Torquay
Surfworld Ocean Art Gallery
Surfworld Museum, Surfcity Plaza, Torquay
Tel. 03 5261 4606

Anglesea
Melaleuca Gallery
121 Great Ocean Road, Anglesea
Tel. 03 5263 1230

Aireys Inlet
Eagles Nest Fine Art Gallery
48 Great Ocean Road, Aireys Inlet
Tel. 03 5289 7366

Lorne
Qdos
Allenvale Road, Lorne
Tel. 03 5289 1989

Skenes Creek
Tanybryn Gallery & Teahouse
Skenes Creek Road, Tanybryn
Tel. 03 5237 6271

Apollo Bay
Dixons Gallery
Shop 1/22 Pascoe Street, Apollo Bay
Tel. 03 5237 1243

Warrnambool
•Warrnambool Art Gallery
165 Timor Street, Warrnambool
Tel. 03 5559 4949

•Customs House Gallery
Gilles Street, Warrnambool
Tel. 03 5564 8963
•Saltmarsh Studio Gallery & Cafe
49 MacDonald Street, South Warrnambool
Tel. 03 5561 7727

Port Fairy
•Wishart Gallery
19 Sackville Street, Port Fairy
Tel. 03 5568 2423
•Whalebone Gallery
39A Bank Street, Port Fairy
Tel. 03 5568 2855

Portland
Portland Arts Centre
Cnr Glenelg & Bentinck Streets, Portland
Tel. 03 5522 2301 or 03 5522 2263

SWIMMING POOLS

Lorne
Lorne Foreshore (outdoor)
Tel. 03 5289 1152

Colac
Bluewater Fitness Centre (indoor, heated)
Tel. 03 5231 4398

Apollo Bay
Apollo Bay Community Pool (outdoor, solar heated)
Tel. 03 5237 6155

Port Campbell
Timboon Swimming Pool (outdoor, solar heated)
Tel. 03 5598 3285

Warrnambool
Aquazone (indoor & outdoor, heated)
Tel. 03 5559 4500

Portland
Leisure Aquatic Centre (indoor & outdoor, heated)
Tel. 03 5521 7174

WEATHER: TEMPERATURES & RAINFALL

Air Temperature: The average temperature along the coast ranges from 13°C in winter to 23°C in summer, however temperatures in the mid to high 30's are not uncommon during summer. The local saying of getting four seasons in any one day is also quite apt.

Rainfall: Annual rainfall ranges from 650mm east of the Otway Ranges to 900mm west of the Otways and is fairly evenly distributed throughout the year. The Otways, however, get most of their 1200 to 2000mm during winter and spring.

Water Temperature: Ranges from 12°C – 13°C in winter to 19°C – 20°C in summer. Waves are generally bigger in winter, but swell is plentiful throughout the year, especially west of Cape Otway.

BACKPACKER & YOUTH HOSTEL ACCOMMODATION

Queenscliff
The Queenscliff Inn YHA
59 Hesse Street, Queenscliff 3225
Tel: 03 5258 3737

Torquay
Bells Beach Lodge
51-53 Surfcoast Highway, Torquay 3228
Tel: 5261 7070

Anglesea
Anglesea Backpackers
40 Noble Street, Anglesea 3230
Tel: 03 5263 2664

Lorne
Great Ocean Road Backpackers YHA
10 Erskine Avenue, Lorne 3232
Tel: 03 5289 1809

Erskine River Backpackers
4 Mountjoy Parade, Lorne 3232
Tel: 03 5289 1496

Apollo Bay
Eco Beach YHA
5 Pascoe Street, Apollo Bay 3233
Tel: 03 5237 7899

Cape Otway
Bimbi Park
90 Manna Gum Drive, Cape Otway 3233
Tel: 03 5237 9246

Princetown
The 13th Apostle
Lot 5 Post Office Road, Princetown 3269
Tel: 03 5598 8062

Port Campbell
Port Campbell Hostel
18 Tregea Street, Port Campbell 3269
Tel: 5598 6305

Port Campbell Ocean House Backpackers
32 Cairns Street, Port Campbell 3269
Tel: 03 5598 6223

Warrnambool
Warrnambool Beach Backpackers
17 Stanly Street, Warrnambool 3280
Tel: 03 5562 4874

Backpackers Barn
90 Lava Street, Warrnambool 3280
Tel: 03 5562 2073

Port Fairy
Port Fairy YHA
8 Cox Street ,Port Fairy 3284
Tel: 03 5568 2468

Portland
Bellevue Backpackers
133 Sheoke Road, Portland 3305
Tel: 03 5523 4038

Cape Bridgewater
Cape Bridgewater Coastal Camp
1721 Blowholes Road, Cape Bridgewater 3305
Tel: 03 5526 7267

Contact Park Offices or Visitor Information Centres for detailed brochures and maps of walking tracks. Parks Victoria offers the following useful advice.

• A reasonable walking rate for adults is 3 to 4 km per hour along level formed tracks. A total of six hours on the track, including rests, is a comfortable limit for a day's walk.

• Three people is the minimum advisable number for a bushwalk. In an emergency this allows one to stay with an injured person and one to go for help.

• Be aware that during nesting season some native birds may swoop. Most birds swoop only during the nesting and rearing period. They are only trying to protect their territory, nests, eggs and young. Most swooping behaviour is a form of bluffing. Birds rarely make contact when swooping.

• Let someone responsible know your plans and your estimated return time. Make sure you tell them when you return safely.

• Ensure that you know the route. Carry an appropriate map. Check directional, warning and advisory signs. If you have a mobile phone, remember that it may not receive or transmit in some areas.

• Carry appropriate gear in a small day pack. For any walk of more than a kilometre or so, take water, a snack and a small first aid kit. Insect repellent and a torch can prove to be very useful. Carry a coat and/or jumper if it's likely to be wet or cold. Several thin layers are better than one or two thick ones.

• Wear suitable footwear such as runners or lightweight hiking boots. Thongs or sandals are not suitable.

• Always wear a hat and use sunscreen in summer. On days above 30°C carry ample drinking water, and have frequent small drinks and rests. Wear a woollen hat in winter; a great deal of heat is lost from the head.

• If you see a snake, don't panic. Stand still or stamp. Snakes nearly always move away when they feel footstep vibrations. Don't attempt to kill it - you could well be bitten, and snakes are protected in any case.

• When walking on the beach or on rocky shores, look out for sudden unexpected large waves. Take great care near cliff edges, and below cliffs. Many cliffs are unstable. Remember that walking on sand can be quite slow and tiring. Check tide times before attempting beach sections.

• Be careful of falling branches on windy days in forest.

• Leeches can be a problem in wet forest. Avoid them by wearing long trousers tucked into socks or gaiters. If one does attach, a match or salt applied to its tail will quickly dislodge it.

• If you encounter a flooded stream change your route, walk upstream or turn back. Don't attempt to cross a fast-flowing stream over thigh deep.

There are three significant and lenghty walks along the south west coast of Victoria:

Surf Coast Walk

A 34 kilometre walk mostly along the coast, and at times the beach, starting at Jan Juc and finishing at Moggs Creek Picnic Ground. It can be easily intercepted at Bells Beach, Point Addis, Anglesea and Aireys Inlet and broken up into shorter legs.

Great Ocean Walk

A 91 kilometre walk from Apollo Bay to Glenample Homestead (near the 12 Apostles). Most of the walk is within the Great Otway and Port Campbell National Parks, taking in key attractions such as Cape Otway Lighthouse, Johanna Beach, Castle Cove, Moonlight Head and Wreck Beach. It includes beach, clifftop and inland-forest sections and has been designed so that walkers can step on and step off the trail at a number of places, completing short day or overnight hikes. There are 7 hike-in campsites and 4 drive-in campsites, or local accommodation is an option. Overnight hikers must register their walking and camping intentions with Parks Victoria on 131963 (or via the internet) at least a fortnight in advance. Camping fees apply. Walkers that camp must move in an east to west direction. Licensed Tour Operators offer guided tours for walkers.

Great South West Walk

A 250 kilometre looped walk between Portland and Nelson. From Portland it heads north-west and inland through forest towards Nelson via the Lower Glenelg National Park. A good part of this is along the spectacular Glenelg River. From Nelson it returns to Portland following the beach or sea-cliffs of Discovery Bay (a 55km beach section), Bridgewater Bay and Nelson Bay. There are 16 campsites evenly spaced along the route specifically for walkers, as well as Parks Victoria campsites that must be booked through the Portland or Nelson information centres. The walk can be broken up into shorter sections of varying lengths.

Point Addis
•Ironbark Basin Nature Reserve
There are 3 walks, including a Nature Trail and a Koori Cultural walk as well as picnic tables.

Aireys Inlet
•Cliff Top Walk
A 2.5km walk between the lighthouse and Sunnymeade Beach
•Distillery Creek Picnic Ground
A variety of bush walks originate from this location.

Moggs Creek
•Moggs Creek Picnic Ground
There are several bush walks at this spot.

Lorne
•Erskine Falls
A short walk, but many steps.
•Sheoak Picnic Ground
A variety of walks lead to a variety of waterfalls including Henderson Falls, Kalimna Falls, Sheoak Falls, Wonwondah Falls and Phantom Falls.
•Blanket Leaf Picnic Ground
A 4km return walk to the Cora Lynn Cascades.
•Cumberland River
Several lengthy walks commence at the camping ground, one goes to the Cumberland Falls.

Wye River
5km circuit walk through bush and back along the beach.

Kennett River
•Grey River Reserve Picnic Area
Located 5 or 6km up the Grey River Road.
•Carisbrook Falls
Located 7km southwest of Kennett River. The short walk starts from the Great Ocean Road at Carisbrook Creek.

Apollo Bay
•Paradise Picnic Reserve
•Marriners Falls
A 3.5km walk along the Barham River
•Marriners Lookout
A short, but steep 20 minute return walk.
•Shelly Beach Picnic Ground
Located about 7km southwest of Apollo Bay, with several walks, one to the beach.
•Maits Rest
A short walk through rainforest (wheelchair access).

Cape Otway
•Blanket Bay Picnic Ground
Several walks originate and pass through this spot.
•Cape Otway Lightstation
The lightstation precinct itself requires a degree of walking between points of interest. There is also a much longer walk to Station Beach and Rainbow Falls.

Aire River
•Aire River Camping & Picnic Ground
There is a 2km walk to the ocean along the river.

Johanna
•Johanna Beach Walk
Goes along the beach to Dinasaur Cove & Rotten Point.

Lavers Hill
•Triplet Falls
A 2km, 40 minute circuit walk, with picnic facilities.
•Otway Fly Treetop Walk (03 5235 9200)
A privately owned company located on 225 acres of cool temperate rainforest 500 metres above sea level. The steel structure is a 600 metre long walkway, 25 metres above the forest floor. The entire walk takes about one hour and admission is charged. The visitor centre includes a gift shop and restaurant.
•Hopetoun Falls
A short walk, but many steps.
•Beauchamp Falls
A 2.5km return walk starting from a picnic ground.
•Melba Gully Picnic Ground
Famous for its rainforest walk, glow worms and the Big Tree.

Moonlight Head
•Wreck Beach Walk
A short walk and 380 steps to the beach where shipwreck anchors lie embedded in the reef.

Princetown
•Gellibrand River Estuary Walk
A walk beside the estuary leads to the ocean.
•Glenample Homestead Picnic Area

WALKING TRACKS, WATERFALLS & PICNIC GROUNDS OF NOTE

Port Campbell National Park
•Loch Ard Gorge
A series of themed walks link the various attractions within the precinct.
•Port Campbell Discovery Walk
Sensational walk along the cliffs of Port Campbell Bay, especially on dusk.

Peterborough
•Bay of Martyrs Walk
A short walk that starts at the Bay of Martyrs carpark.

Childers Cove
There are several walks in this remote area.

Warrnambool
•Lady Bay Foreshore Promenade
Part track and part boardwalk that stretches 6km between the Breakwater and Logans Beach Whale Nursery.

Warrnambool cont.
•Tower Hill State Game Reserve
There are 4 walks, picnic facilities, abundant native fauna and a visitor centre located in this old volcano.

Port Fairy
•Griffiths Island Walk
A 2km walk that takes in the muttonbird colony and lighthouse.
•Mahogany Trail Walk
A 22km beach walk between Port Fairy and Warrnambool.

Mount Eccles National Park
There are 4 walks and picnic facilities located around Lake Surprise, a volcanic crater.

Portland
•The Great South West Walk
See earlier description.

Cape Nelson State Park
•Cape Nelson Lighthouse Walk
The walk starts at a picnic area.
•Sea Cliff Nature Walk
A 3km circuit walk. Numbered pegs along the track are explained in the Park Notes for the walk.

Cape Bridgewater
•Seal Colony Walk
A 5km return walk along high seacliffs to view the seals at the very end.
•The Blowholes and Petrified Forest
Very short walks take you to and connect these two attractions.

Discovery Bay Coastal Park
•Swan Lake Sand Dunes
Make your own tracks through the massive dunes which are very accessible from the camping ground at Swan Lake.

USEFUL INTERNET SITES

Parks Victoria (National, State & Coastal Parks)
www.parkweb.vic.gov.au
Coast Action/Coastcare (Summer by the sea activities)
www.dse.vic.gov.au/coasts
Geelong Otway Tourism
www.geelongotway.org
Shipwreck Coast Tourism
www.shipwreckcoast.com.au

Tourism Victoria
www.visitvictoria.com
The Great Ocean Road
www.greatoceanrd.org.au
The Great Ocean Walk
www.greatoceanwalk.com.au
The Great South West Walk
www.greatsouthwestwalk.com

Swellnet (Surfing forecasts, surfcams etc.)
www.swellnet.com.au
Surfing Australia (governing body for surfing)
www.surfingaustralia.com
Bureau of Meteorology
www.bom.gov.au
Otway Ranges Environment Network
www.oren.org.au

About one third of the coastline between Port Phillip Heads and the South Australian border is national, state or coastal parkland. This is a crucial factor in preserving the unique nature of the glorious landscape through which the Great Ocean Road sweeps. Victoria's parks are areas of land permanently set aside from sale or development to protect their natural and cultural values. At each of the parks, information sheets describing points of interest and walking tracks are obtainable from a Parks Victoria office or Visitor Information Centre. The walks suggested on the sheets are always described in detail with maps. Camping is permitted in the majority of parks. Domestic animals and firearms are prohibited in all the parks, however, in the case of dogs there are some exceptions. The overriding one is that it is acceptable for dogs to be left in the car whilst their owners are visiting the sights, but only in the course of travelling through a park via a main road, such as the Great Ocean Road. Fires may be lit only in fireplaces provided, or as directed by signs. No fires at all may be lit on days of Total Fire Ban. All native plants and animals, all geological features and all historical and cultural remains are protected by law in parks and must not be disturbed or removed. On the other hand, though, rubbish must be taken from a park when leaving. There are ten Marine National Parks and Marine Sanctuaries along the Victorian southwest coast. Sites for these parks and sanctuaries have been chosen to ensure that a system representative of Victoria's diverse marine habitats is protected for the future. To achieve this the parks have been spread across Victoria's

five marine bio-regions. Commercial and recreational fishing is not permitted in the Marine National Parks or Marine Sanctuaries, nor is other extractive or damaging uses such as aquaculture, exploration drilling, oil and gas extraction, dredging, or waste disposal. Access for recreation, tourism, education and research within these areas is generally unrestricted, although subject to permit in some instances. Marine communities in Australia's southern waters are unique, with around 90% - 95% of the plants and animals found nowhere else on earth. Just as National Parks are set aside for the preservation of natural environments on land, there is also the need to protect areas in the sea to keep safe special marine environments. The Marine National Parks System is designed to contribute to the long term ecological viability of marine and estuarine systems, maintain ecological processes and protect marine biodiversity.

GREAT OTWAY NATIONAL PARK

The Great Otway National Park incorporates the former Otway National Park and Angahook-Lorne, Carlisle and Melba Gully State Parks, as well as areas of State forest and other Crown land. The new national park covers 103,000 hectares, an increase in park area of more than 60,000 hectares. This park represents all that is special about the Otways: the tall wet forests, ancient rainforests, the drier forests of the inland slopes and the very diverse heathlands and woodlands, fringed by a spectacularly rugged coastline and studded with some of Victoria's most striking waterfalls and

other attractions. The Park begins at Anglesea and follows the spine of the Otway Ranges all the way to Moonlight Head. Properly described in the main part as a cool temperate rainforest, its vegetation, however, ranges from tall mountain forests to heathland and wetlands. The Park boasts an abundance of waterfalls and a network of well made and clearly signposted walking tracks. Many follow old timber tramways used in logging days. Beautiful picnic grounds in forest settings, all with good facilities, are plentiful. The Park's numerous coves and sandy beaches are often characterized by rock platforms between sand and sea, ideal for ocean fishing. Equally, swimming, surfing, horse riding and scenic drives can all be pursued in the most exhilarating of environments. Overall, the Park has one of the most diverse floras in Victoria and the drier part, around Aireys Inlet, includes heathland with abundant wildflowers in spring and early summer. This locality is especially renowned for its native orchids. The heathlands are also good areas for bird-watching, with more than 150 species of birds recorded in the park. The Park's diverse habitat provides for a wide range of wildlife with many opportunities to catch a glimpse of them in their natural surroundings. At night, owls, gliders, possums and bats can be spotted. The Otways is also home to the uncommon but unique and threatened Spot-tailed Quoll. At the eastern end of the Park, around Lorne, bushfires are a natural occurrance during the scorching summer months and significantly shape the forest. The last major fire was Ash Wednesday in 1983. Fire continues to play a vital role in forest ecology, influencing plant and animal diversity. At the other end of the Park, however, the Otways have the highest rainfall in the state, in places over 2000 millimetres annually. The rainforest is best known for its towering mountain ash, one of the world's tallest trees, growing up to 100 metres high, and so coveted by loggers. (Native forest logging in the Otways is legislated to cease in 2008, whereas plantations will continue on private land.) Maits Rest, just out of Apollo Bay, is the most accessible place to feel the rainforest. It is a popular, well signed, forty minute walk, with sections of raised boardwalk to keep the feet dry. Tree ferns abound and giant mountain ash soar. Another spot to experience the rainforest is Melba Gully, located just west of Lavers Hill. The original property was named after Dame Nellie Melba and donated to the state in 1975. Early in the century there were two sawmills operating in the gully and during the 1930s and 40s tea-rooms on the property provided a popular tourist stop-over and picnic spot. The current picnic ground is on the site of the tea-rooms and is provided with wood BBQs and toilets. Leading off from this open area is a looped nature walk taking about 35 minutes to complete. The walk passes through a gully of thick forest comprising myrtle beech, blackwood and tree ferns, with an understorey of low ferns and mosses. It has a lot in common with the Maits Rest Track, but is darker and even more saturated. At night it becomes quite atmospheric while viewing the glow worms for which the park is most famous. They are actually a species of small fly at the larval stage of growth and make sticky threads that trap insects attracted by their glow. Wooden bridges along the track cross the Johanna River, cascading in parts, and at the top of a set of steps is the Big Tree, a messmate some 300 years old and 27 metres in girth. Triplet Falls is the third spot that Parks Victoria has invested heavily in as a significant rainforest experience. It has been recently upgraded from an 800 metre walk to that of two kilometres. It includes elevated walkways and now passes through old forest and beside beautiful cascades below the main falls. There are also picnic facilities. About ten minutes further along the Beech Forest Road are Beauchamp Falls and Hopetoun Falls, the latter probably being the most dramatic waterfall in the Otways. Nearby is Turtons Track, a rainforest drive down a very windy road. From here you can get back to the Great Ocean Road via the equally enthralling, but much wider Skenes Creek Road. Although the Great Ocean Road, turns inland at Apollo Bay, the Great Ocean Walk provides an alternative route, for the more robust. (see Walks & Waterfalls page 70) Otherwise, access to the coast (still within the National Park) after Apollo Bay requires a few deviations The first and essential turnoff is to Cape Otway and the lighthouse. Blanket Bay is on the way and worth the detour to take in its beauty. Westward of Cape Otway, along the coast, the National Park becomes a narrow strip of significantly varying terrain, all the way to Princetown. There are turnoffs to the Aire River Estuary, Johanna Beach and Moonlight Head, all popular, yet remote attractions within the Park. There are about 20 camping sites spread throughout the Park and numerous picnic grounds, usually attached to walking tracks and waterfalls. Camping fees apply only to the Blanket Bay site and then only during peak periods when booking is required.

PORT CAMPBELL NATIONAL PARK

Stretching from Princetown to Peterborough, Port Campbell National Park is a mostly narrow strip of coastal heathland lying between the Great Ocean Road and the sea, just 1750 hectares in area. It is its edge and interface with the sea, though, that makes it spectacularly unique. Best known for the Twelve Apostles island rock formation, the park boasts numerous other spectacles of nature etched into the limestone cliffs, in places providing sheer drops of 70 metres. The coast's formation began around 10-20 million years ago. Countless millions of tiny marine animal skeletons built up beneath the sea to form limestone. As the ocean retreated the soft limestone was exposed to the wild seas and pounding winds of the Southern Ocean. Over millions of years the sculpting of rock stacks, gorges, islands, arches and blowholes has inexorably taken place. Ironically this constant erosion is both a destroyer and creator. It is the agent by which headlands become islands, rock stacks and arches, but also the cause of their ultimate destruction when they collapse. Sometimes slowly, sometimes dramatically. There are always rock falls eating away the cliffs, but occasionally an icon suddenly vanishes. The most recent was that of one of the 12 Apostles collapsing in a heap on Sunday 3rd July 2005.

Prior to that one of London Bridge's arches collapsed in 1990. Loch Ard Gorge is famous for the wreck in 1878 of the Loch Ard, a three-masted clipper wrecked off Mutton Bird Island with the loss of 52 lives. The island is named for its rookery of Muttonbirds (Short-tailed Shearwaters), migratory birds that can be seen returning to the island each night at dusk, between September and May. Nearby are the Blowhole, Loch Ard Cemetery and Thunder Cave, all linked by themed walking tracks that connect to Loch Ard Gorge. Both the Twelve Apostles and London Bridge have fairy penguin colonies, each isolated and protected by the cliffs. At dusk they return in their hundreds from a day of feeding and can be seen from the excellent viewing platforms. (These are very much in keeping with a tradition of inspired wooden structures, for access and viewing, all the way along the Great Ocean Road.) On exposed clifftops, grasslands and heathlands stunted by the effects of salt-laden winds, dominate the fragile soils. Though they are often bleak looking, a surprisingly large range of birds and animals inhabit them. Southern Brown Bandicoots, Echidnas, Eastern Grey Kangaroos and Swamp Wallabies and the rare (but not around here) Rufous Bristlebird, to name but a few. Skyward there are Peregrine Falcons, Wedge-tailed Eagles, Australasian Gannets, and Wandering Albatrosses. Gibson Steps Beach is adjacent to the 12 Apostles and one of the few accessible beaches in the park. Access is by way of steps cut dramatically into the vertical cliff face, zigzagging down to the sandy beach below. Down the road a bit is the same Mr. Gibson's

pioneer homestead, Glenample, built in 1869 and open to the public. It houses a comprehensive display of the Loch Ard Shipwreck, along with other local history. There is also a picnic ground. At Port Campbell the Discovery Walk along the cliff's edge, beside the bay, takes in spectacular views all the way to Two Mile Bay, where shell middens are evidence of Aboriginal occupation and their long association with the coastline. Camping in the park is only allowed at the Port Campbell Caravan Park, very nicely located near the beach.

BAY OF ISLANDS COASTAL PARK

The Bay of Islands Coastal Reserve was reclassified as a Coastal Park in 1996 to better reflect its conservation value and more adequately cope with its high visitor frequency. Perhaps not as spectacular as its close neighbour the Port Campbell National Park, it has, however, a dynamic succession of sheltered coves and sandy beaches that are a lot more inviting and accessible. The Park stretches 33 kilometres as a long, narrow strip from Peterborough towards Warrnambool and is only 800 hectares in area. Vegetation is coastal heathland and home to the Rufous Bristlebird. Usually heard more than seen, this endangered species flits around, mostly on foot, under cover of vegetation. The heathland is colourful in spring when Yellow Banksias, Pink Swainson's Pea, Pig Face, Golden Groundsel and Purple Flag Lilies are flowering. The two main attractions are at the Peterborough end of the Park: the Bay of Martyrs and the Bay of Islands. Both of these bays are scattered with numerous rock stacks and

islands, some serving as predator-free sanctuaries to various seabirds such as Silver Gulls and the rare Black-faced Cormorant. A short interpreted walks goes from the Bay of Martyrs carpark to Halladale Point where the Falls of Halladale was wrecked in 1908. Folklore has it that a group of local Aboriginals were slaughtered by early European settlers in this area, thus the names Bay of Martyrs and Massacre Bay which is nearby. There are, however, no documentary records of the incident. Further to the west, and closer to Warrnambool, are Childers Cove and adjacent Murnane Bay. They are fairly remote, being well off the main road, but perfect for beach walks or a picnic. Camping is not permitted in the Park, however, there is a camping ground close by at Peterborough.

TOWER HILL STATE GAME RESERVE

Tower Hill was formed 25,000 years ago when hot rising basaltic magma came into contact with the sub-terranean water table. The violent explosion that followed created the funnel-shaped crater, now a lake, and islands seen today. This idyllic formation was preserved in its original beauty in an oil painting by Eugene von Guerard in 1855 (now hanging in the Warrnambool Gallery). Sadly, by 1861 much of the land had been cleared of timber, and as natural vegetation disappeared so did the birds and mammals. Moves to protect the area resulted in Tower Hill being declared Victoria's first national park in 1892, becoming a state game reserve in 1961. Using von Guerard's painting as a blueprint, a unique experiment in revegetation and wildlife recolonization began in 1961 to recreate an environment destroyed by man. Over 300,000 trees and shrubs have been planted, enticing back the birds and providing a new home for the mammals reintroduced. There are now emus, koalas, kangaroos and echidnas roaming around, the emus definitely being the most friendly. A series of short walks take visitors around the reserve and there is a picnic ground with electric BBQs. The Natural History and Visitor Centre includes displays of the local geology and revegetation program. It was designed by Robin Boyd and is managed by the Worn Gundidj Aboriginal Cooperative. Founded in 1992, the cooperative is a not-for-profit organization which combines contemporary artistic creation and nature based tourism with traditional knowledge. Camping is not permitted in the reserve.

MOUNT ECCLES NATIONAL PARK

This national park is like a huge oasis in the midst of vast tracts of farmland. The focus of interest is Lake Surprise, comprising three adjoining volcanic craters fed by underground springs. Clinging to the craggy cliffs surrounding the lake is a woodland of manna gums and blackwoods. The craters beneath the lake were formed as a result of volcanic activity some 20,000 years ago. The most recent eruption was less than 7,000 years ago, suggesting to volcanologists that it may not be completely extinct. Although Mount Eccles is 180 metres above sea level it appears more a hill than a mountain and was formed by lava exploding from the crater, solidifying into scoria and being blown

eastwards. Aboriginal tribes resided in two areas around Mount Eccles - one area south of the park at Lake Gorrie, the second at Lake Condah, west of the Park. They constructed stone huts in both areas and stone fish traps at Lake Condah, and lived on fish, native plants and animals. They were permanent residents in these areas until European settlement slowly pushed them out. Blackwood, Austral Bracken and Manna Gum (a koala's favourite food source) are the most predominant species of vegetation. The park has a series of beautiful bush walks, parts of which are accessible to wheelchairs. The Crater Rim Nature Walk can be demanding in parts, but rewards walkers with the best views. There is also a large lava cave, so take a torch. Camping sites and picnic facilities are provided.

CAPE NELSON STATE PARK

Cape Nelson State Park is a relatively small park, 11 kilometres south-west of Portland, at the tip of a headland covered in coastal scrub and heathland. Its geographic prominence was cause for the location of its splendid lighthouse and surrounding compound, built in 1884 and open to the public. Many native animals can be found in the Park including rare and threatened species such as the Heath Mouse, Swamp Antechinus and Rufous Bristlebird. More common animals include the Red-necked Wallaby and Echidna. The many bird species found include wrens, honeyeaters, rosellas and Bronze Wing Pigeons. They are particularly noticeable during spring when the rich smell of Soap Mallee nectar is in the air. This small tree is part of the reason

the park exists; to protect a plant species otherwise only found in South Australia. The area is accessible via Cape Nelson Road or the more interesting Scenic Road, off which is a picnic area with views of the lighthouse in the distance. The Great South West Walk follows the Cape's coastline along its craggy limestone cliffs. There is also a three kilometre Sea Cliff Nature Walk including points of interest described in park notes. Camping is not permitted.

DISCOVERY BAY COASTAL PARK

Just before Tarragal on Bridgewater Lakes Road, it is worth pulling over to take in the extraordinary vista of the sand dunes of Discovery Bay Coastal Park. They are an amazing expanse, several kilometres wide in places, stretching from the South Australian border eastwards along the full length of Discovery Bay. A distance of approximately 55 kilometres. The dunes have expanded somewhat since cattle grazing and rabbits have removed vegetation, but natural erosion has also played a part and they are now a mass of mobile sand, forever shifting. Behind them are a series of small lakes, reedy swamps and heathland. At Descartes Bay the Park narrows to only a few hundred metres in width following the cliffs (and path of the Great South West Walk) around to Cape Bridgewater and Bridgewater Bay. This section includes the spectacular Blowholes when a large sea is running. Unfortunately, owing to the collapse of tunnels in the volcanic rock many yeras ago, they no longer create their once sensational cannonlike effects. Very close

NATIONAL PARKS, STATE PARKS & COASTAL PARKS

by is the Petrified Forest. This curiosity was supposedly formed when a forest of Moonah trees was smothered by a large sand dune, creating unusual sandstone formations around the decaying tree trunks. Around the corner is a seal colony located at the base of 130 metre high cliffs flanking Bridgewater Bay. Discovery Bay Coastal Park is excellent for observing bird life along the vast stretches of sandy beach. The Park is an important habitat for the endangered Hooded Plover and many other waders migrating from overseas. Another spot for observing birdlife is the estuary at Nelson where spoonbills, pelicans and swans can be seen. Camping sites are located at Swan Lake and Lake Moniebeong, close to the sand dunes.

LOWER GLENELG NATIONAL PARK

Flowing through the greater part of the park is the Glenelg River, "the finest body of fresh water I have seen in Australia", as the Surveyor General of New South Wales, Major Thomas Mitchell, wrote in 1836, on his historic expedition down the river. For 15 kilometres along its lower reaches, the river has carved out an impressive gorge through limestone, with cliffs 50 metres high. Typical of areas with a limestone geology, there are many caves in the vicinity, but only the Princess Margaret Rose Caves are open to the public. They are over 20 metres underground, 150 metres long and have an amazing array of stalactites and stalagmites. Surrounding the caves and display centre is a glorious parkland with walks along the Glenelg River and a picnic and camping ground. Upstream are a further 17 campsites, eight of which are accessible by car, the remainder only by canoe or walking. These camps are an integral part of the Great South West Walk, which follows the river closely. The Glenelg River is perfect for canoeing, which is an ideal way of observing the park's rich birdlife, especially the waterbirds. The native animals, though sometimes difficult to find, include rare species such as Swamp Antechinus, Potoroos and small colonies of wombats. The Park has an impressive range of plants, over 700 species in all, including 50 orchids and a dazzling display of wildflowers found amongst the heathland at the eastern end.

MOST ACCESSIBLE RAINFOREST EXPERIENCE & NATIVE ANIMAL ENCOUNTERS

Apollo Bay - Great Otway National Park
• Turtons Track (drive)
• Miats Rest (walk with wheelchair access)

Lavers Hill - Great Otway National Park
• Triplet Falls (walk & picnic ground)
• The Otway Fly (elevated treetop walk)
• Melba Gully (walk & picnic ground)

Koalas
• Grey River Road at Kennett River
• Sausage Gully, near Grey River on the Great Ocean Rd
• Otway Lighthouse Road, Cape Otway
• Tower Hill State Game Reserave

Kangaroos
• Anglesea Golf Course
• Tower Hill State Game Reserve, near Warrnambool

Emus
• Tower Hill State Game Reserve

Seals
• Little Henty Reef at Marengo near Apollo Bay
• Lady Julia Percy Island, Port Fairy
• Cape Bridgewater

Southern Right Whales
• Logans Beach, Warrnambool between May & October

Penguins
• London Bridge (PCNP) viewing platform at dusk.

Waterbirds
• Swan Bay, Queenscliff
• Barwon River Estaury, Barwon Heads
• Breamlea wetlands
• Aire River Estuary, near Glenaire
• Gellibrand River Estaury, Princetown
• Curdies River Estuary, Peterborough
• Muttonbirds on dusk between September and April at Griffiths Island, Port Fairy and Muttonbird Island at Loch Ard Gorge in the Port Campbell Natioanl Park
• Gannet colony at Point Danger, Portland

By the close of the 18th century exploration of Victoria's coast was underway. In the early 1800s the French and English were almost shadowing one another's vessels in the quest to chart the area and gain advantage for future claims. The most remarkable effort though, was by Matthew Flinders and George Bass. Unbelievably, these two dedicated navigators made initial explorations in a mere dinghy, 2.5 metres long, and aptly named the Tom Thumb. Although they did not venture far from Sydney Harbour, the experience was sufficient to prepare Bass for a voyage of nearly 1,000 kilometres to Western Port Bay in an open whale-boat. Successively larger vessels took them further afield with each journey and resulted in progressively more significant discoveries, in particular that of the strait between Victoria and Tasmania eventually named after Bass. Its discovery reduced sea-passage from England by a week. The earliest settlements along the south-west coast followed the landcalls of whalers and sealers, at their seasonal outposts around Warrnambool, Port Fairy and Portland. Whaling flourished until the 1840s, then began to wane as over-hunting exhausted supply. At the same time a shortage of land in Tasmania and the ever increasing number of immigrants to the colony, prompted pastoralists to stake their claims in the rich hinterland between Geelong and Portland. By the middle part of the century, the rush for gold turned the flow of immigrants into a flood. Bound for Melbourne and Geelong, an endless stream of ships passed close by the south-west Victorian coast. All too often, too close. Over 150 ships lie wrecked between Port Phillip Heads and the South Australian border. In time, a flourishing network of coastal traders was established, plying the waters with supplies for the settlements, and providing passage to Melbourne. For travellers the voyage from Warrnambool, at about two days, was immeasurably quicker than the overland route, though a little more hazardous at times. Whilst whaling and sealing was the catalyst for settlement along the coast west of Cape Otway, timber was a more important factor to the east. The Otway Ranges were considered to have some of the best timber in the colony. The mountain ash were massive, soaring over 100 metres with trunks up to six metres in diameter. There was variety as well as size, including bluegum, spotted gum, messmate, stringybark, ironbark, blackwood and beech. Apollo Bay and Lorne were the only two bays able to provide safe anchorage on the coast bordering the Otway Ranges. Apart from providing passing ships with supplies and shelter from rough conditions, they became focal points for a timber industry that flourished in the area during the 1850s and 1860s. However reliance on inefficient sea transport saw a shift of activity to the inland. Demand for timber, as well as land for settlers, naturally grew in the 1860s and 1870s as the colony became more populous. Unfortunately, though, around this time a great deal of timber was wasted when bush was burned by settlers taking up allotments. There was an urgency by farmers to clear land and make it productive, but it was largely inaccessible to loggers. This latter problem was overcome by the establishment of a network of tramways, especially around the towns of Forrest and Beech Forest, allowing the industry to gather pace. The tramways were a narrow gauge, mostly timber track, and the trucks were drawn either by horse team or steam locomotive. Unfortunately none of the tracks have survived the ravages of time and bushfire. In the period 1850 to 1950 approximately 300 timber mills were established, a mobile mass of machinery that moved around the Otways, relocating every two or three years to new stands of timber. Lorne and Apollo Bay remained isolated settlements, reliant on the sea for supplies despite the possibility of overland travel growing more feasible in 1859, when a telegraph line was established linking Tasmania with Melbourne. The cable passed through Geelong and Winchelsea, as a telegraph wire above ground, then turned south to Moggs Creek. From there it followed the coast all the way to the telegraph station at Cape Otway, then crossed Bass Strait under the sea via King Island. However, for the most part, the track following the mainland coastal section was only traversable by foot or horse. The first proposals for an ocean road between Geelong and Lorne came about in the 1880s, but were defeated because defence authorities thought it might make the area vulnerable to invasion. The establishment of the Country Roads Board (CRB) in 1912, and its subsequent commitment to employ returned servicemen from World War One for road construction proved to be a great stimulus. The government recognized that little had been done to adequately service the numerous, and often economically significant, settlements along the south west coast of Victoria. In 1916 the CRB proposed a road starting at Barwon Heads travelling all the way along the coast to Peterborough, where it would connect with existing roads continuing on to Portland. The project received government endorsement, not only for the obvious economic reasons, but in large part because the Minister of Public Works saw the added potential for it to serve as a tourist attraction of international interest. The final impetus, however, for realization of the project came from community support and resulted in the formation of the Great Ocean Road Trust in 1918. Influentially, it included members of both state and local government and the CRB. Funds were raised and planning commenced as a private enterprise. After a year spent surveying its intended route, construction then started on the first section between Lorne and Cape Paton in 1919, carried out by the CRB for the Trust. Progress was slow and arduous in the extreme, especially for the thousands of returned soldiers employed, many of them debilitated by war. For the most part, tools of construction were picks, shovels and crow bars. Some suggested prison labour might be more appropriate for the task. The section from Eastern View to Lorne was opened in 1922, with a toll applied to vehicles using it, and in 1932 the entire stretch between Anglesea and Apollo Bay was completed. However, the next section behind Cape Otway remained a snaking dirt road for many years, preventing completion of the whole project until the 1980s. The Memorial Arch at Eastern

RIGHT: 1874 studio portrait of aboriginals by JW Lindt.

View was originally built in 1939 with a plaque bearing the inscription: "the road was built to commemorate the services of those who served in the Great War". Owing to fire, tempest and a misguided truck, the arch has been rebuilt several times since, most recently in 1991. In 1932 the Great Ocean Road was regarded as a significant engineering achievement. The consequences were enormous for the townships dotted along its route, especially as foreseen, in the area of tourism, for the road was in fact the creation of a coastal scenic drive that rivalled any in the world.

ABORIGINAL HISTORY IN WESTERN VICTORIA

Apart from the heavily forested and sparsely inhabited areas of the Otway Ranges, the Aboriginal population density throughout south-western Victoria was one of the highest anywhere in Australia. Their total number in the Western District alone was approximately eight thousand. By 1840, though, only six years after first settlement in Victoria, an invasion of over 10,000 Europeans had swept across the rich agricultural land of the Western District, and the collapse of Aboriginal society was well underway. Originally, aborigines in this area had lived in small nomadic groups numbering between thirty and one hundred, and moved between sites located around lakes, marshes and rivermouths that provided plentiful supplies of food and fresh water. The composition of these groups was always changing, principally for the purpose of marriage. Numerous small groups in a particular area constituted a tribe, and tribal boundaries were determined by economic, geographic and cultural factors, however, generally there were no distinct natural borders. South-west Victoria had five or six such divisions, each with different languages and various dialects within them. Interaction, whether at a group or a larger tribal level, usually concerned sharing food resources and was greatest during seasons of abundance. For example, gatherings of up to 1,000 people occurred during whale strandings near Port Fairy and large scale hunting drives were often organized. Populations tended to be higher along the coast than inland owing to a wider variety and more plentiful food sources. Fish, eels, stranded whales and shellfish enriched the more standard inland fare of possums, koalas, echidnas, emus and kangaroos. (Many shell middens or mounds are still in evidence today along the coast.) Ceremonial occasions and the trading of raw materials or implements also drew the smaller groups or tribes together, though these meetings were also where hostilities might flare up. Generally relations in the Western District were more friendly than competitive, owing to an even distribution and relative abundance of resources. Closer to Geelong this may not have been the case. According to William Buckley's accounts hostilities between bands seemed to be incessant, though usually aroused by squabbles over females. First European contact with the aborigines involved gifts such as beads, mirrors, rugs and tomahawks, irresistible charms designed to ingratiate. These were also offered in exchange for land and naturally the aborigines tried to obtain as much of this novel material wealth as possible.

LEFT: Rickety saw mill tram near Apollo Bay, circa 1890.
RIGHT: Road building near Cumberland River in 1906.

However, as settlement advanced and consumed their land, they no doubt felt defrauded by the inequity of the situation, and justified in raiding stations for food, clothing and livestock. But the reprisals were devastating. If a European happened to be killed during such a raid, brutal massacres of entire Aboriginal camps invariably followed. Another factor in the rapid population decline was that of foreign diseases, as well as the problem of many women being abducted and prostituted, resulting in sterility from venereal disease. Several Aboriginal missions were established in the 1860s in the Western District. One at Lake Condah, near Mt. Eccles National Park, contains the remains of stone houses constructed by the Aboriginals thousands of years ago. Another mission at Framlingham, near Warrnambool, has become a trust operating as a co-operative and today houses about one hundred Aboriginals who farm 2,000 acres in the district.

WILLIAM BUCKLEY – "THE WILD WHITE MAN"

In 1803 William Buckley, aged 23, escaped from a short-lived convict settlement at Sorrento and spent 32 years dwelling with the local aborigines around Geelong and the coast. At 6 feet 6 inches, he cut an impressive figure, but his chances of surviving in the bush were considered so slim that it gave rise to the expression "Buckley's Chance!". The following narrative (held in the Manuscripts Collection of the Latrobe Library) was given by Buckley to George Langhorne, two years after ending his nomadic life. "I remember very little of my early years. I was born at Tiverton in England where my uncle Buckley resided when I left England, but my parents had removed sometime previous to my departure. I was apprenticed to a bricklayer from whom I ran away and enlisted into the regiment of foot, but changed into the fourth, or King's Own Regiment, when that regiment was ordered to Holland in 1799, with the troops under the command of the Duke of York. On my return I met with the misfortune which occasioned my being sent out a prisoner to New South Wales. One day crossing the Barrack Yard where our regiment was quartered a woman whom I did not know requested me to carry a piece of cloth to a woman of the Garrison to be made up. I was stopped with it in my possession, the property had been stolen, I was considered the thief and though innocent, sentenced to transportation for life. In the year 1804, I believe, I arrived here in the Calcutta where it was proposed to form a colony upon some part of the coast, though this design was afterwards abandoned. Dissatisfied with my condition as a prisoner of the Crown and finding that the ship was about to sail for Van Dieman's Land I resolved to make my escape and if possible find my way overland to Port Jackson. I made known my plan to two other prisoners and we all three succeeded in cutting away a boat and making our escape in her to the shore, where we left her to her fate and ran up the country. We pursued our way up the Port as far as the Yarra River until near where Melbourne now stands and having by this time consumed the small stock of provisions we brought with us. We left a tea kettle and other articles behind us on the bank and struck into the bush. I wished to direct our course to the northward in hopes by so doing to reach Sydney which I believed was not far off.

Here we differed and my two companions taking one direction, I took the other, when however I had gone some little distance my heart failed me and in a desponding frame of mind, I again directed my steps towards the sea and at length reached the Heads of the Bay in a state of considerable exhaustion for afraid as yet to eat all the wild berries that came in my way, not being acquainted with their properties and supposing some of them poisonous. I subsisted principally on crawfish, suffering much from thirst. On reaching the coast I in vain looked for the ship, it had probably been gone some time. Up to this period I had not seen any of the natives, but at length I fell in with an old black fishing near the sea with his wife and a large family of children. By this savage I was treated with the greatest kindness, partook of their food and laboured with them. I gradually became capable of expressing my wants in their language. I left this old man and wandered further into the country and then fell in with several more families of blacks. Our meeting took place thus – I was sitting under a tree near a lagoon, not far from the River Barwin, dispirited and almost worn out with my sad condition, when some black women made their appearance. I learnt afterwards that they had come hither to gather to gather the gum from the mimosa tree, which forms a favourite article of food. I had been I believe about two months resident in the country, but I do not think they had heard of me. On seeing me they retired and informed their companions who were nigh at hand. These came up and viewing me for some time with evident astonishment at length made signs to me to follow them. I immediately did so although I despaired of my life as my impression was that they intended to kill me. They took me to to their encampment, one black holding one of my hands and one the other. On reaching a hut or 'willum', near which was a waterhole, I made signs that I was thirsty and they gave me some water and without being asked offered me some gum beat up and prepared after their manner. They then all sat down and a general howling was set up around me, the women crying and sobbing and tearing their faces and foreheads with their nails. A token of excessive grief, I learnt afterwards, that they believed me to be a black who had died some time since, and who had come again to them in the shape of a white man. In the evening a great dance took place. I believe in honour of my arrival, and from this time I was to them an object of the utmost care and solicitude. They never allowed me to walk any distance unattended, and if I happened to leave them for a little, blacks were immediately sent in search of me, when tears were often shed on my reappearance. I lived as they lived and was careful not to give them offence in the smallest thing, yielding to them at all times and sharing with them whatever I took fishing or in the chase. They gave me a black woman for a wife, but observing that this occasioned jealousy among others of them I relinquished her to the native and contented myself with being single. This seemed to please the men much, and I was no longer apprehensive of danger from them. I had lived about six months with them when

LEFT: Split Point Lighthouse at Aireys Inlet, ca. 1915.
OPPOSITE: "The Finding of Buckley" by Oswald Rose Campbell, 1869 - courtesy of the Geelong Art Gallery.

I fell in with one of my companions whom I found living with some blacks on the sea coast. He then came and lived with me, but from his faithless conduct to the blacks and dissolute behaviour towards their women, I was so apprehensive of danger to us both that I resolved to part from him, and I therefore told him that it was necessary for our mutual safety that one must leave the tribe. He left and I never heard of him more, except by a vague report that he had been killed by the blacks. This fate I felt assured from his imprudent conduct awaited him. My other companion I never heard of after parting from him at the Yarra It is probable he met the same fate as the former and perhaps on the same account. I now made up my mind to continue with the tribe (Watourongs) and principally lived about the River Barwin, my favourite place of

abode being the part now called Buckley Falls. I soon lost all reckoning of time. I think after I had been about two years in the country, I soon after was enabled to express myself in the black's language pretty well, so as readily to make known my wants and after a few years residence among the natives I could speak the language quite well. When I had attained this knowledge of their tongue I found I was fast losing my own. My situation, however, was now less irksome as I was able to converse with them, respecting themselves and their connection with the different tribes. The subject of religion I was careful not to introduce, as I was afraid that they would kill me if I meddled with their customs or superstitions. I have frequently entertained them when sitting around the camp fires with accounts of the English people, houses, ships, great guns etc., to which

accounts they would listen with great attention and express much astonishment. The affection of the tribe for me always remained the same. If I hinted at the probability of some day or other rejoining my own countrymen they manifested grief and shed tears. As I always kept up at night the best fire and had the best 'miam miam' in the camp (the blacks notwithstanding cold being often too lazy to attend to their fires) the children would often prefer to sleep with me and I was a great favourite among them. On one occasion feeling uncomfortable from the dirty state in which I was (it was soon after I had joined them), I repaired to the lagoon before mentioned to wash myself. Thinking I had run away from them as I had not mentioned my intention, they were presently engaged in searching for me. An old man named Bow...t., on discovering me among the reeds, took me out by the hand and immediately burst into tears. They appeared overjoyed at having found me and ever afraid lest I should again leave them. When engaged in their fights which were very frequent when I first came among them, I was always obliged to accompany them, but never compelled to take a part. They would arm me with a spear and place me aside in some bush or other concealment, but if discovered by the opposing party I was never disturbed or attacked. The wars between the Waworong and Watourongs have been numerous and bloody. I have accompanied the latter in their night expeditions against the former when, falling suddenly upon their camp, they have destroyed without mercy

LEFT: Port Campbell Bay and settlement, circa 1912.
OPPOSITE: Family outing in the Otways, circa 1890.

men, women and children. I have sometimes succeeded in parting them when about to fight. I became as expert as any of them in spearing the kangaroo and taking fish, and with regard to the latter was generally more successful when fishing alone. My practise was to light a fire as a signal to the blacks in the neighbourhood to come and partake of my spoils which they never failed to do. Besides the kangaroo, o'possum, bandicoot and sugar squirrel, they seek with great eagerness for the hedgehog, or porcupine which forms a delicious article of food. In order to obtain it from its hiding place they put into the hole a young child with its legs foremost, who feels how and where the animal is situated and reports accordingly in what part he is to be obtained by digging into the earth, as the holes run under and parallel with the surface for some distance. Their method of dressing it when obtained is this: they enclose it entire in a piece of bark and thus roast it, then taking off the skin again apply the body to the fire. Thus dressed it is considered a great treat. I have noticed at least four different tribes who speak as many different dialects. The family, or portion of the tribe, with whom I spent the greatest part of my time was called the Wattewarre. In their wars I observed one circumstance worthy of notice, should they happen to lose their spears, they make afterwards but faint efforts and appear to give all up for lost. It is true they are cannibals. I have seen them eat small portions of the flesh of their adversaries slain in battle. They appeared to do this not from any particular partiality for human flesh, but from the impression that by eating their enemies they would themselves become more able warriors. Many of them are disgusted with this

ceremony and refusing to eat, merely rub their bodies with a small portion of the fat as a charm equally efficient. They eat also of the flesh of their own children to whom they have been much attached, should they die a natural death. When a child dies, they place the body in an upright position in a hollow tree and allow it to remain there until perfectly dry, when they will carry it about with them. On the subject of religion, as I said before, I never conversed with them. I do not believe that they possess any distinct notion of a Supreme Being, or of the Soul or Spirit. I have heard them warn their children not to frequent the neighbourhood of a grave, otherwise I have not observed that they have any superstitious dread of particular places. There are, however, two imaginary Beings whom they treat with a certain degree of respect. One of these is supposed to reside in a certain marsh and to be the author of all the songs which he makes known to them through his sons. The other is supposed to have charge of the pole or pillar by which the sky is propped. Just before the Europeans came to Port Phillip this personage was the subject of general conversation. It was reported among them that he had sent a message to the Tribes to send a certain number of tomahawks to enable him to prepare a new prop for the sky as the other had become rotten and their destruction was inevitable should the sky fall on them. To prevent this and to supply as great a number of iron tomahawks as possible, some of the blacks repaired to Western Port and stole the iron work from the wheels of the sealer's cart. It is about 25 years since I first saw a European tomahawk among them. On enquiring where they obtained it, they informed me that while I was absent some distance in the interior, some white men had rowed up the Barwin in a boat and had left the tomahawk at the place where they landed. On visiting the spot I observed the place where the strangers had dug to procure water. The native tomahawks (merang) are made of talc shaped in an oval form and placed in a bent stick, the two ends of which, are firmly bound together. A syphilis disorder is very prevalent among them, attacking not only the adults but the children. Promiscuous intercourse of the sexes is not uncommon, and in certain festivals is enjoined. At certain times the women are lent to the young men who have not wives. The women in other respects are faithful to their husbands. Sometimes a black will go to a willam or a miam miam to entice a woman away. Should the husband be within, he will give permission to her to follow him and on her return will probably snatch a fire brand from the fire and beat her severely. During thirty years residence among the natives I had become so reconciled to my singular lot that, although opportunities offered, and I sometimes thought of going to the Europeans I had heard were at Western Port, I never could make up my mind to leave the party to whom I had become attached. When therefore I heard of the arrival of Mr. Batman and his party, it was some time before I would go down, as I never supposed I could be comfortable among my own countrymen again."

LEFT: The doomed "Falls of Halladale", a 2085 ton, 275 feet long barque wrecked near Peterborough in 1908. RIGHT: Festivities on the Moyne River, Port Fairy, 1915.

Edward Henty is officially regarded as establishing the first European settlement of Victoria at Portland in 1834. However, William Dutton, a whaler and sealer who frequented the waters off the south-western coast in the 1820's was perhaps Victoria's first pioneer, given that he occasionally resided in a hut that he built in Portland during this time. Reports of his whaling exploits are reproduced here from the Portland Guardian.

24.6.1843 – Just before the closing poll on Tuesday last, and as the electors had nearly all recorded their votes, as if to revive the declining excitement of the day, a whale presented herself in front of the town, and literally, but unobservedly came alongside of the 'Essington'. The schooner's boats were manned as soon as thought of, and before the men had got fairly seated on their thwarts they were fastened to the forward fish, and were towed along in gallant style. The whale, however, dissatisfied with the treatment, and galled by the cold iron embedded in its body, resisted, and with its flukes swamped the boat, plunging the crew in the water, and breaking the left leg of one of the men, named Samuel Hundrel, rescued itself from its bondage. Another boat, which belonged to the 'Prince of Denmark,' immediately fastened, but with similar success. Dutton, in the meantime, was looking on to see the sport, and panting to participate in the fray, when suddenly the chance occurred, and the 'Rampant Lion' was on the back of the sea monster. The iron took secure hold, and not withstanding the ponderous rolling and the fearful attitudes which at times the huge creature assumed, the practised hands which at last it fell into, were prepared for all its movements. After repeated strokes of the lance,

and loss of blood, it gradually became weak and ceased to struggle. The unfortunate man's leg is severely fractured below the knee, and he now lies at the Commercial Inn, attended by Dr. Sutherland, in a very precarious state.

8.6.1844 – A valuable addition to the wealth of the district and the colony, has been made during the week, in the capture of two good sized fish. On Tuesday, one of the most animating and enchanting scenes, of the kind, occurred that has ever taken place in the bay. A chase of two hours was given on the approach of two spouters which were destined to assist the prosperity of the successful parties. A line of boats could be distinctly seen from the town, gliding through the undulating waters, the oars glittering in the sun at every stroke, as if tipped with burnished gold; and the

hardy and determined spirits which were wielding them, making the briny waters at each tug appear as though the boats were flashing fire. It was only by dint of hard pulling that the fish were overtaken. Hector Wales with a praiseworthy ardour to secure the prey, disregarding his own safety and that of his crew, met with a severe accident, in the destruction of his boat. The whale upon which he pulled was fierce; it struck his boat with its flukes, throwing at the same time the whole crew overboard, and as though the monarch of the deep felt the insult of being pursued and approached with so little ceremony, wreaked its vengeance on the sunken vessel, till neither keel nor a plank was left entire. Fortunately no other accident occurred, and eventually both wales were captured.

Perhaps the most famous shipwreck in Australia, the three-masted clipper Loch Ard met her fate in the early hours of June 1st, 1878, when swept onto a reef extending from Muttonbird Island. Eva Carmichael (travelling with her parents and five siblings) and Tom Pearce, were the only survivors and the following is Eva's account of her ordeal. "I left Gravesend on 2nd March as a passenger on board the iron ship 'Loch Ard'. There were 52 souls on board in all, and alas! poor Tom Pearce and I only are left out of that number. We had a splendid passage, having encountered but one half gale when west of the Cape of Good Hope. We were indulging the hope of a prosperous voyage, but it is remarkable that Reginald Jones had a dark foreboding of disaster. He often told me that he had a presentiment that he should never plant foot on Victorian soil, and I have repeatedly endeavoured to dispel his fears, which, alas! have been verified, for I am afraid 49 have perished with him. The 'Loch Ard' struck against a rock between 5 and 6 o'clock on Saturday morning. The concussion was alarmingly loud, and threw us all into confusion and terror. Every time she struck the rock afterwards a streak of light, probably caused by friction, flew upwards like a gleam of lightning. The masts, blocks, and yards falling on every side rendered it impossible for the crew to lower the life-boats which were made fast. There were 5 life-buoys and 6 life-belts on board, and I succeeded in getting one of the latter. Captain Gibb, in the midst of the rushing to and fro, chanced to see me and shaking me by the hand, exclaimed 'If you should be spared to see my dear wife, tell her that I stood to my ship to the last, and went down with her like a sailor.' Poor Captain Gibb, I don't think he tried to save himself. In a minute or two afterwards I found myself in the sea, contending with the waves. One of the strings attached to my life-belt broke, and the belt shifting up and down forced my head under the water several times, which almost cost me my life. Seeing a hencoop I swam towards it. God taught me to swim in my distressed plight; for I never swam before. I succeeded in getting hold of the hencoop, and so did Arthur Mitchell. This hencoop had been an object of ridicule among the passengers on board; but I felt thankful for it in the water. By this time the ship had disappeared under the waves. Seeing a spar, I let go the hencoop and made for it. In a few minutes Mitchell and Jones were clinging to the spar also. Mitchell began to shiver frightfully, and to despair of ever reaching the shore. He had a life-belt; but poor Jones kindly took off the life-buoy which was around himself and put it round Mitchell. Mitchell asked me to give him some of my clothing to keep the wind from piercing him: I tried to do so, but I could not divest myself of my Jacket, having to hold onto the spar with one hand. Poor Jones and Mitchell soon let go the spar; and, after swimming some little distance they disappeared. I was now left alone, and could see nothing but the waves rolling and a rock at a little distance. I let go the spar and made for it. The waves dashed me against the rock, and then sent me spinning round its point. I went down under the waves three or four times, and began to despair of life. In a few minutes after turning the point of the rock, I saw Tom Pearce standing on the beach. I shouted to him, whereupon he walked into the water and swam towards me. Tom had a desperate struggle to bring me ashore; and from the time I shouted to him to the time we were safe on the beach about an hour must have elapsed. He took me into a wild looking cave, a few hundred feet from the beach, and finding a case of brandy which was washed ashore, broke the neck of one of the bottles and made me swallow almost all its contents, after which he swallowed a drop himself. Cold and exhausted – for we must have been in the water about five hours – we lay down on the ground. I soon fell into a state of insensibility, and must have been unconscious for hours. When I awoke Tom Pearce was not to be seen. Cold, weak, and terrified, with the wild waves before me, and caves and steep hills around me, I hoped God would send some one to deliver me. After what seemed a long time, I heard a strange noise. It proved to have been the cooeying of Mr. Gibson; but being a stranger to this kind of noise, I imagined it to have been the war-cry of the aborigines. I was afraid to answer, and remained silent for a while, when I heard some one say 'Yes!' I thanked God when I heard that English word, and was instantly in the company of Mr. Gibson and a young man. Mr. Gibson took off his shoes and stockings and put them on me, wrapping me in blankets. A fire was soon lighted, coffee made, and brandy procured. I felt my strength somewhat recruited; but for all that, felt feeble and helpless, and sore with the bruises which I had received from collision with the rocks and floating wreckage. In the darkness of the night two young men, under the superintendence of Mr. Gibson, conveyed me up a steep and lofty precipice. I cannot understand how they succeeded in bringing me to the top. It must have been a work of great difficulty and danger. Mr. Gibson put me into his buggy, and drove onto his house, arriving there after one o'clock on Sunday morning. Mrs. Gibson has tended me like a mother. Were it not for her constant kindness and sympathy, I should die."

1. **Queenscliff Lighthouse**
   Built: 1863
   Height: 24 metres

2. **Point Lonsdale Lighthouse**
   Built: 1902
   Height: 21 metres
   Tours - 03 5258 3440

3. **Aireys Inlet Lighthouse**
   Built: 1891
   Height: 34 metres
   Tours daily - 03 52631133

4. **Cape Otway Lighthouse**
   Built: 1848
   Height: 20 metres
   Tours daily - 03 52379240

5. **Warrnambool Lighthouse**
   Built: 1858 on Middle
   Island, now at Flagstaff Hill.
   Height: 9 metres
   Open daily

6. **Port Fairy Lighthouse**
   Built: 1859
   Height: 12.5 metres
   Tours - 5568 2682

7. **Portland Lighthouse**
   Built: 1859 at Battery
   Point, moved in 1890 to
   Whalers Point.
   Height: 12 metres

8. **Cape Nelson Lighthouse**
   Built: 1884
   Height: 32 metres
   Tours 131963

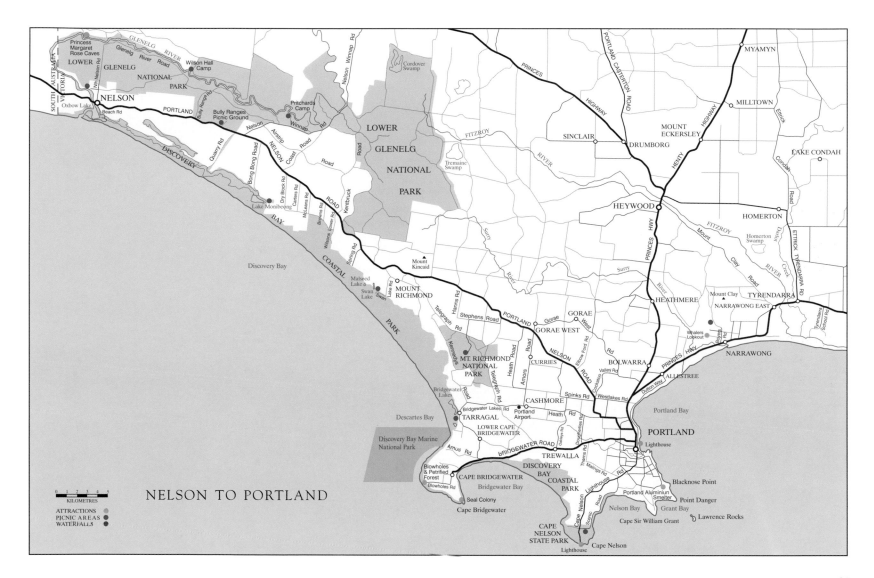

NELSON TO PORTLAND

KILOMETRES
0 1 2 3 4 5

ATTRACTIONS
PICNIC AREAS
WATERFALLS

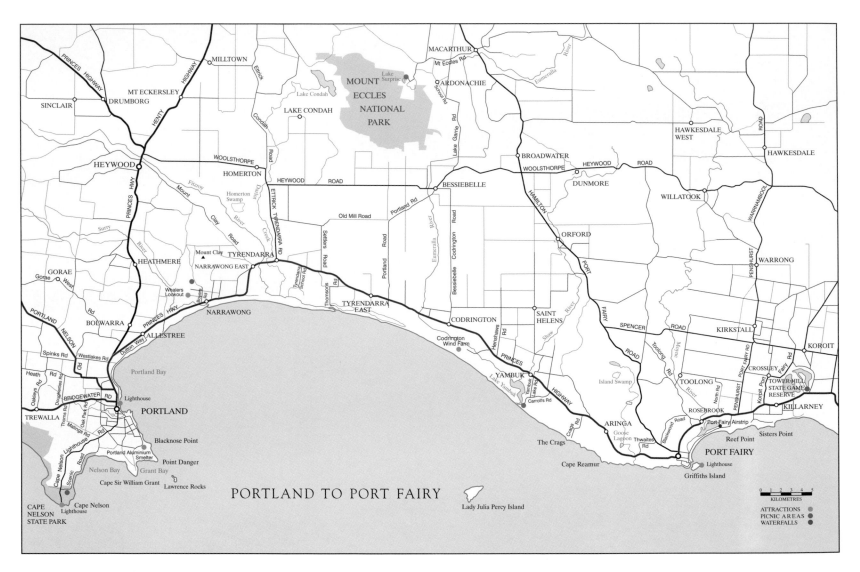

PORTLAND TO PORT FAIRY

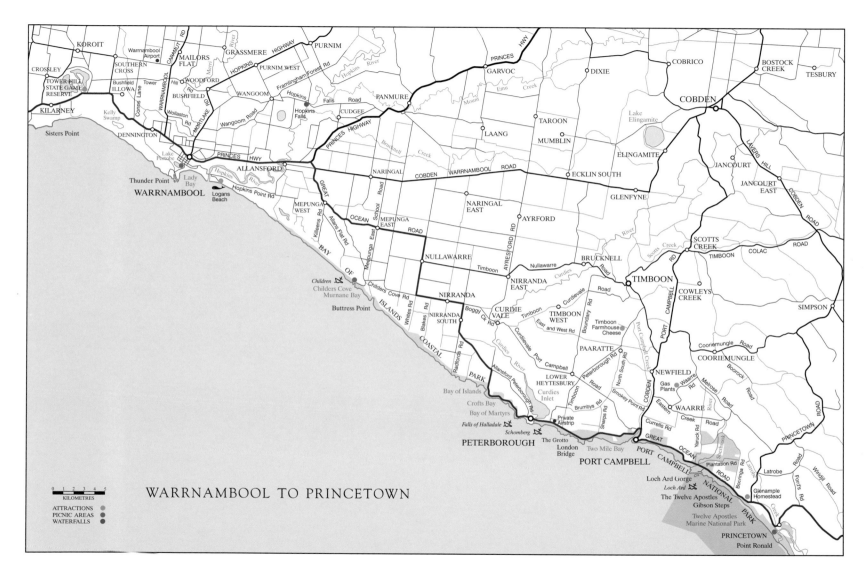

WARRNAMBOOL TO PRINCETOWN

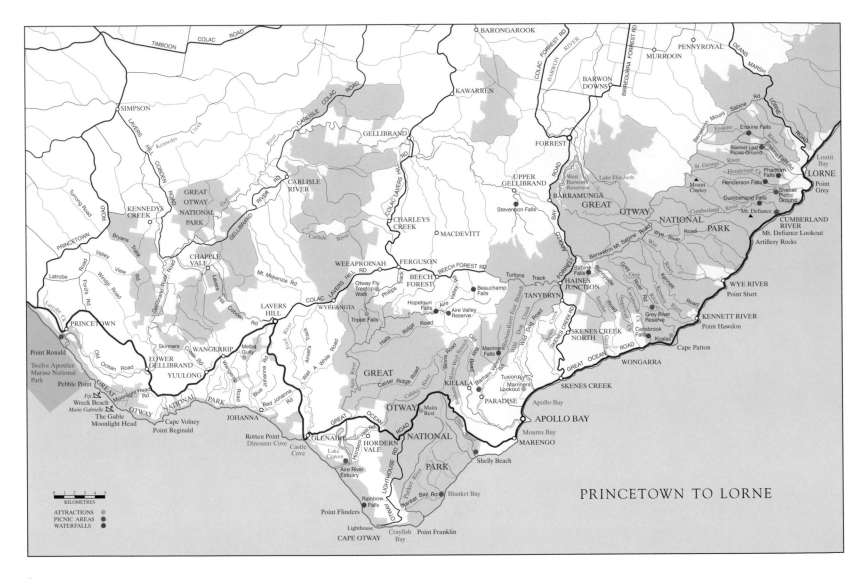

PRINCETOWN TO LORNE

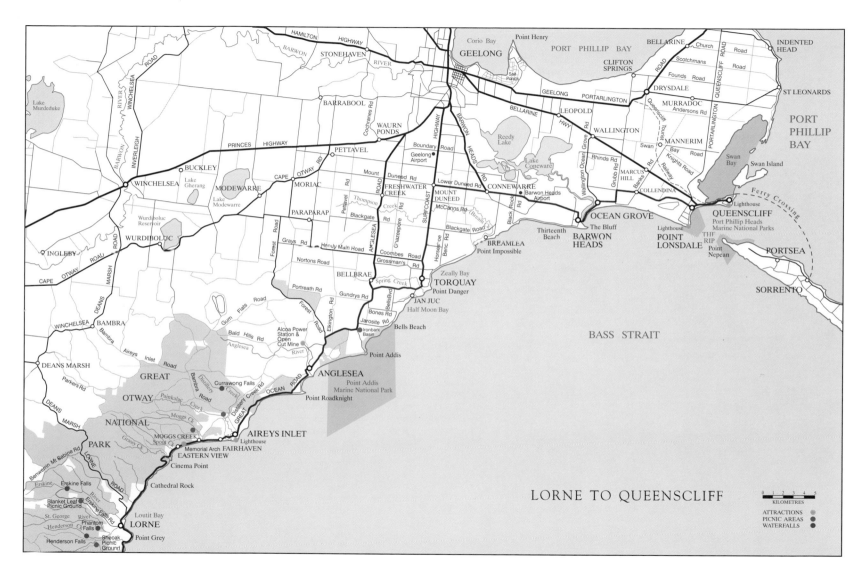

LORNE TO QUEENSCLIFF

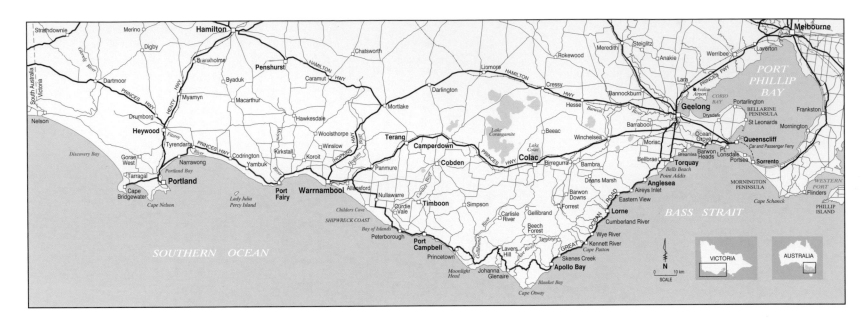

Published by Great Ocean Publications
120 Currells Road, Port Campbell, Victoria 3269, Australia
Phone & fax: 61 3 5598 6203   Email: rodneyhyett@bigpond.com

First Edition 2003, Second Edition 2007
Photographed, written and designed by Rodney Hyett
© Rodney Hyett 2003, 2007

Printed in Singapore by Imago

ISBN 978 0958 6573 58